Danes and Icelanders in Michigan

Danes and Icelanders in Michigan

Howard L. Nicholson, Anders J. Gillis,
and Russell M. Magnaghi

Michigan State University Press

East Lansing

♾ The paper used in this publication meets the minimum requirements of
ANSI/NISO Z39.48-1992 (R 1997) (Permanence of Paper).

Michigan State University Press
East Lansing, Michigan 48823-5245

Printed and bound in the United States of America.

20   19   18   17   16   15   14   1   2   3   4   5   6   7   8   9   10

LIBRARY OF CONGRESS CATALOGING-IN-PUBLICATION DATA
Nicholson, Howard L.
Danes and Icelanders in Michigan / Howard L. Nicholson, Anders J. Gillis, and Russell M. Magnaghi.
pages cm. — (Discovering the peoples of Michigan)
Includes bibliographical references and index.
ISBN 978-1-61186-094-8 (pbk. : acid-free paper)—ISBN 978-1-60917-386-9 (ebook) 1. Danes—
Michigan—History. 2. Icelanders—Michigan—History. I. Gillis, Anders J. II. Magnaghi, Russell M.
III. Title.
F575.S19N53 2013
305.893'9810774—dc23
2013010292

Cover and interior design by Charlie Sharp, Sharp Des!gns, Lansing, MI
Cover photograph is courtesy of the Flat River Historical Society, Greenville, Michigan.

Michigan State University Press is a member of the Green Press Initiative and is
committed to developing and encouraging ecologically responsible publishing
practices. For more information about the Green Press Initiative and the use
of recycled paper in book publishing, please visit *www.greenpressinitiative.org.*

Visit Michigan State University Press at *www.msupress.org*

Dedicated to
Michigan's Danish and Icelandic immigrants
and their descendants.

Contents

Acknowledgments

This work was made possible through the generous assistance provided by the helpful staffs of the Danish Immigrant Archives at Grand View University, Des Moines, Iowa; the Burton Historical Collection at the Detroit Public Library; the Flat River Historical Society and Museum, Greenville, Michigan; the Manistee County Historical Museum, Manistee, Michigan; the Marquette Regional History Center, Marquette, Michigan; the Mason County Historical Society and Historic White Pine Village, Ludington, Michigan; and the White Cloud Michigan Community Library, White Cloud, Michigan. Throughout Michigan there were countless individuals who graciously shared their family files and materials, which greatly enriched the story. Aaron Reider, a Northern Michigan University pre-med student and now alumnus, provided invaluable service in the editing process for which the authors are grateful.

The Icelandic story demanded a create-and-search spirit. We are indebted to Halldor Egilsson of Menominee, Michigan—and the only Icelandic immigrant in the Upper Peninsula—for his insightful oral interview. From Winnipeg, Manitoba, Canada, Audrey Juve Kwasnica, associated with the Icelandic-Canadian newspaper *Lögberg-Heimskringla*, was extremely helpful, as were numerous archives and library staffs, even when telling us the information did not exist. We are indebted to everyone and thank them all.

Finally, we would like to acknowledge Arthur W. Helweg, professor emeritus at Western Michigan University, who was the impetus who got this series, Discovering the Peoples of Michigan, rolling and ultimately this volume in print. This small volume is a milepost on the road to understanding the Danes and Icelanders in Michigan.

Preface

We created a combined history of Danish and Icelandic immigrants who came to Michigan in large part because Icelanders came to the state in very small numbers and were not listed as a separate national group in the United States census until 1930. Since Iceland was part of Denmark through much of the period covered in this book they were often counted as "Danes." As a result, it is difficult to identify Icelanders through census records. These two ethnic groups started to immigrate to Michigan in significant numbers in the 1850s and they continued to do so well into the twentieth century. Key individuals and events are used here to illustrate the larger picture. An examination of Danish religious, educational, and fraternal organizations provides a basis for appreciating the struggles and successes of Michigan's Danes. An overview of Icelandic history and its connection with Denmark is also presented along with the immigration process. Although the number of Danes and Icelanders was small, those who settled in Michigan could readily interact with other Scandinavian peoples—Norwegians and Swedes—whose languages and cultures were similar. As collective groups they experienced increased economic prosperity and integration into the American milieu.

Danes in Michigan

Howard L. Nicholson and Anders J. Gillis

Introduction

Danish immigrants have played an important role in Michigan's develop-ment.[1] Danes generally integrated smoothly into the American fabric and became successful and productive citizens. Compared to Swedish and Norwegian immigration, Danish immigration to America was a stream rather than a mass exodus. From 1820 to 1905 an estimated 225,000 Danes emi-grated.[2] Very few early Danish Americans settled in Michigan. In 1850 there were thirteen Danish-born persons in Michigan; by 1870 there were 1,354; and in 1890, there were 6,335. Danes were always a small number in terms of the larger Scandinavian immigration. They dispersed across Michigan with concentrations found in Detroit, Greenville, Manistee, and Menominee. A large percentage of the Danish immigrants were single men seeking work, land, and opportunity. Forty-one percent of Danish immigrants from 1868 to 1900 were unmarried men. During this period Danes primarily worked blue-collar jobs; however, they soon transitioned to higher management positions. They also played pivotal roles in the development of Detroit's auto industry.

Danish immigrants came from a rich and proud history. Around the turn of the first millennium the Viking age came to a close when Scandinavia was integrated into mainstream Europe. Denmark emerged as a unified nation in the 1100s, and in 1387 Denmark, Norway, and Sweden entered a tenuous alliance, the Kalmar Union. This joined the Scandinavian countries together under the Danish crown. The union helped facilitate Denmark's supremacy, making it the most formidable Baltic power of the Middle Ages.

Danish power was challenged. The Swedes, led by Gustav Vasa, broke off from the Kalmar Union in 1523. An intense rivalry followed as the former Kalmar Union countries quarreled to control trade, levy tariffs, and impose taxes on the valuable loads of timber and foodstuffs that flowed out of the Baltic region.

In 1660 Denmark transitioned to absolutism, making the monarchy hereditary and even more powerful. Despite monarchical gains, the crown suffered setbacks. During the seventeenth century Denmark surrendered large portions of its territory to the Swedes as a consequence of the Karl Gustav wars. During the Napoleonic Wars, more than a century later, Denmark did not fare much better. Pinched between the great European powers, Denmark chose an alliance with France. The result, as historian Knud J. V. Jespersen noted, was that "Denmark ended up as the biggest loser from the Napoleonic Wars."[3] Denmark's chief loss was Norway. Greenland, Iceland, and the Faroes, however, remained in Danish possession as a testament to Denmark's former might.

Denmark lost more territory to Prussia during the nineteenth century. Domestically, the vestiges of feudalism and a population explosion left arable soil in short supply. Many Danes left rural life to find work in city factories. Employment opportunities, however, did not keep pace with Denmark's growing population. Furthermore, in the 1860s military conflicts, territorial losses, suppression of Danish culture, and threats of conscription from neighboring Prussia convinced many to emigrate.[4] America, including the state of Michigan, was viewed as a place with much promise.

Many of the earliest Danish immigrants to the United States were from eastern Denmark, especially Zealand and Lolland-Falster.[5] After 1885 many of Michigan's Danish immigrants came from Jutland.[6] Danish immigrants frequently left behind parishes where they were fortunate to own a few hectares. Michigan's growing lumber and mining industries and, subsequently, the auto industry provided Danes with many opportunities.

Danish Religion, Folk Schools, and Fraternal Organizations

ducation, social organizations, and religion helped Michigan's Danes maintain their ethnic identity.[7] Danish parents and folk schools used education to create and cultivate an appreciation of Danish culture and language. Danish social organizations fostered and promoted Danish culture by emphasizing holidays and mores. Michigan's Danes were also linked with Denmark through religion, which provided an intellectual, cultural, and spiritual framework.

Danish Religion

Religion was a dominant factor in Danish history and played an important role in the lives of many Danish immigrants. Christianity arrived in Denmark around the eighth century, but the Danes were reluctant to convert and many initially held on to their traditional beliefs. In the twelfth and thirteenth centuries Christianity became the dominant religion. Roman Catholicism was the state religion until the 1530s when Protestantism swept into Denmark from Germany and took over. The 1849 Constitution maintained the Lutheran state church; however, provisions were made for religious freedom and dissent. Fractures soon emerged. In the late nineteenth century the Danish religious landscape was dominated by debates about Lutheran theology; the two major camps were the Grundtvigian and the Inner Mission.

Nikolaj Frederik Severin Grundtvig (1783–1872) was a Lutheran academic and pastor whose thoughts and writings incorporated aspects of classic European liberalism. His willingness to confront other religious figures made him controversial. Nevertheless, many Danes liked his concepts, which blended religion and nationalism. On the other hand, those of the Inner Mission were opposed to Grundtvigian ideas, believing that an overemphasis on nationalism was a needless distraction to Christian living.

The debates between the Grundtvigians and Inner Mission believers pitted revisionists versus traditionalists. For the Grundtvigians the Bible was important but not completely infallible.[8] Furthermore, Grundtvigians felt a strong sense of nationalism, though they often rejected the particular brand of nationalism taught by Denmark's state church.[9] Michigan's Grundtvigian Danes tended to cling more tightly to their Danish heritage than the traditionalists; for example, Grundtvigians were central to the establishment of folk high schools that emphasized Danish language and culture. These schools were usually founded, taught, and attended by people with a Grundtvigian background. Grundtvigians believed that nationalism was in no way a hindrance to their faith and that being a good Christian was essential to being a good Dane.

The Inner Mission toed a tighter line: the Bible was authoritative. Inner Mission followers believed that Grundtvigians overemphasized their nationalistic convictions to the detriment of their faith. Grundtvigians rebutted that the Inner Mission followers were dogmatic. Reconciliation among clergy was difficult. In America the Reverend Peter Sørensen Vig, a devout member of the Inner Mission, and the Grundtvigian Frederik Lange Grundtvig (the son of the famous Danish bishop) engaged in heated polemics. The Inner Mission clergy taught that to reach people Danes needed to go beyond the boundaries of traditional Danish culture. For them, the Grundtvigian school of thought created a subculture of Danishness that made it difficult to proselytize. As a result, the Inner Mission members were more ready to accept Americanization.[10]

Many Danes cared little for clerical quarrels. After interviewing Danes in Montcalm County, Michigan, in the late-twentieth century John Bille noted that "none of them were clear as to what the quarrel was about."[11] Before

1870 most Danes lived in areas where there were too few Danes to form a local congregation, let alone quarrel about complicated doctrinal matters. In such cases, Danes joined other Scandinavian Lutheran churches, as well as Adventist, Baptist, and Unitarian churches among others.[12] In areas where there were enough Danes to fill out a congregation, they often built and supported a local Danish church.

For example, Danes living in Ludington, in Mason County, attended a church where they joined with Norwegians and Swedes until 1878 when they formed Bethany Lutheran Church, an independent Danish congregation. The Ludington Danes relied initially on pastors from Manistee and Muskegon to come and serve the congregation. As the church grew, it became able to support resident pastors, who helped solidify the church as a pillar of Danish culture in the community. The church's Vacation Bible School taught children the Danish language in addition to religion. Many of the church's activities were organized by Danish women. The Ladies Sewing Society, founded in 1887, raised funds and did routine maintenance to keep the church running. Children's Sunday School classes were established by local Danish women, and the Ladies Aid organization made considerable donations to furnish the church's interior.

Danish churches were used as meeting places for civic and charitable organizations. Where Danish churches were constructed ethnic identity was clearly evident and cultural heritage was celebrated. A scarcity of Danish pastors in Michigan, however, sometimes made it difficult for churches to become spiritual and ethnic cradles. Some Danish pastors traveled extensively to serve multiple congregations in different parts of Michigan. In the 1870s Holger Rosenstand, who preached and lived in Manistee County, was one of the only Danish pastors in Michigan. Rosenstand traveled to logging camps to preach to Danish woodsmen. As the nineteenth century progressed, more Danish pastors arrived in Michigan, and Danes became better equipped to break away from other Scandinavian churches.[13]

Many of Michigan's Danes had strong religious convictions. Denmark's history of absolutism and Lutheranism tended to blur the lines between the secular and the divine, helping make the Danish religious experience an encompassing life philosophy. In the accounts left by Michigan Danes, religion repeatedly surfaces as one of the most important aspects of life. Despite doctrinal differences between the Grundtvigians and the Inner Mission,

Danish Baptists in Michigan

The Baptist church first came to Denmark after 1839 when Julius Köbner on the island of Funen was converted to the Baptist faith in Hamburg, Germany. The faith slowly spread throughout the country, which held Lutheranism as its state religion. In the mid-nineteenth century Danish Baptists began to leave due to poverty, religious oppression, or a hope to spread the faith in America. The first Danish Baptist church was established in Pennsylvania in 1855. Immigrant churches were established primarily in Iowa, southern Minnesota, and eastern Wisconsin, and a newspaper, *Oliebladet* (The Olive Leaf), was founded to help communicate and to promote the religion. In Michigan Danish Baptist churches were established at Ludington (1890), Bear Lake (1891), and Edmore (1894). As congregations grew smaller or no longer needed the Danish language for services, many of them merged with American Baptist congregations, as did the church at Bear Lake. The other two were discontinued in 1922 and 1936.

many Danes were unified by Danish churches. Nevertheless, though Danish churches helped bind Danish communities together, not all Danes were religious. It has been estimated that in some areas as few as twenty-five percent of immigrant Danes ever joined an American church.[14] Even where religion was not central to Danish immigrants' lives, it often was on the periphery of education, social organizations, and holidays, making it an important part of Danish culture.

Danish Christmas

Christmas was a special time of the year for Michigan's Danish immigrants in the late nineteenth and early twentieth centuries.[15] They carried with them their rich Christmas traditions centered on family. A popular Danish family tradition was the Advent calendar. The calendar was specifically designed as a countdown to Christmas Day. Danes did much more, however, than just use the calendar. Baking and meal preparation, for instance, frequently started weeks in advance. Vanilla cookies and coffee cake were two recipes that commonly appeared around the holiday season.

The Danish infused Christmas with symbols of folklore, religion, and nationalism. To this day, Danes string up small Danish flags around Christmas. This practice complements the fact that the Danes typically view red and white as the Christmas colors. Red hearts and candles are another Danish favorite around the holidays. Like an Advent calendar, candles are sometimes used to mark the days until Christmas. The candles also serve as a religious symbol. Furthermore, the Christmas tree was adopted early on by Danes, from their southern neighbors, the Germans.

An interesting facet of Danish Christmas is the belief in elf creatures known as Julenisse. According to Danish tradition the playful and troubling elves only stop their mischievous antics after a special treat such as cereal or porridge is left out for them.

Christmas Eve is commonly of more importance than Christmas Day in Danish tradition. Christmas Eve is usually celebrated with a candlelight church service, the ringing of bells, family gatherings, and the finest food. At the end of the main meal rice porridge is served. An almond is placed in the porridge; whoever gets the almond receives some sort of prize, perhaps candy or some special title. As exemplified by the Nielsens of Menominee, the family typically gathers around the Christmas tree, sings carols, dances around the tree, opens gifts, and enjoys one another's company. The tree, traditionally complete with store-bought and homemade decorations and candles, is a delight for the children. Safety, however, mandates that the parents remain vigilant and keep a bucket of water nearby to prevent fire.

A typical Danish Christmas Eve dinner consists of roast goose, a bread dressing with prunes and apples, and, for dessert, apple cake and whipped cream. After dinner the father, or some other close family friend or relative, might dress as the Julemand, a kind of Danish Santa Claus. Gifts are opened one-by-one, giving each person a chance to see what others receive. Beyond the home, additional celebrations and trees were found in the communities with local gymnasiums and churches. According to Alvin Nielsen it was almost a miracle that there were no fires during the gymnasium holiday celebrations that were held during World War I, considering the huge candlelit Christmas trees. As Alvin recalled, men with "long fish poles equipped with wet sponges to put out fires" stood by ready to douse any dangerous flames.[16]

On Christmas Day, Danes made the rounds with family members and close friends they did not get the chance to visit with the day prior. Appetizers were served to the visitors, and toasts were made with aquavit, a caraway seed–flavored clear liquor. Christmas was very festive, and for many Danes the celebration continued into the next day.

The Christmas holiday season was an especially important time of the year for Danish immigrants in the late nineteenth and early twentieth centuries because they were reminded of their roots. To the immigrants from Denmark the colors, candles, folklore, and food were visible symbols of their Danish heritage.

The Danish Folk School

Nineteenth-century developments in Danish religion were closely linked to education reforms.[17] Early nineteenth-century reforms entitled young Danes to an education.[18] Later in the nineteenth century, folk schools in Denmark became an important part of education reform. The first Danish folk school in the United States was established in Elk Horn, Iowa, in 1880, and a school opened in Michigan two years later in Newaygo County.

Folk schools were founded on the teachings of the theologian, philosopher, and poet N. F. S. Grundtvig. They combined Lutheranism and nationalism. Grundtvig's ideas were simple yet revolutionary; he believed education should exist, "to make every Dane an enlightened and useful citizen."[19] Grundtvig, who eventually became a bishop, maintained that an emphasis on education and Danish culture helped Danes experience true spiritual enlightenment. The Danish folk school developed from this belief.

N. F. S. Grundtvig's folk school concept was driven by a love for the common person. Grundtvig adopted new insights and concluded that education should not be monopolized by the elite. As a result, he created folk schools for ordinary citizens. Some have suggested that this was an important step in moving Denmark from absolutism to democratic political reforms. Furthermore, folk schools celebrated Danish history and culture while providing an outlet for Danish nationalism. This was important because Danish nationalism was bruised by war and territorial losses to Prussia during the nineteenth century.

The movement to establish Danish folk schools in America began early. In 1876 Danish Lutheran ministers met in Chicago and proposed the idea. Their desire to have a folk school constructed in Chicago was never fulfilled;

however, their vision did take root in Iowa and Michigan, through the efforts of an ordained minister named Hans Jørgen Petersen. Petersen came to the Grant area in 1882 with the intention of building a school, which would turn out to be the only Danish folk school established in Michigan. Petersen had arrived in America in 1875, and in 1880 he had helped open and operate the first and most successful Danish folk school in Iowa, of which he was president until 1882. He had high aspirations for its Michigan counterpart.

Various locations were discussed by Petersen, but Peter Kjolhede, a minister from Muskegon, intervened. As a result the school was built some thirty miles northwest of Grand Rapids near Grant in Newaygo County. The decision was motivated by the desire to minimize the land costs, but the location later made it difficult to recruit students.[20]

Before the school was established there were very few Danes in Ashland Township. The first Dane there, Martin Jensen, arrived in 1876; most of the other Danes who followed shortly thereafter had already been living in Michigan or came directly from Denmark.[21] A tract of farmland was purchased from Timothy Murphy, and the Danes in the area eagerly went to work constructing the school on that site.

When the school opened in 1882 it was christened Ashland Folk High School. It, like other Danish folk schools, did not require entrance examinations or set any other academic requirements for enrollment. Furthermore, the school did not issue diplomas or certifications. Students appreciated the lack of stringent examinations and course requirements. They studied the Bible, history, and the Danish language in a peaceful atmosphere. In 1919, one of the school's students, Ellen Anderson, said of the school: "Here we listen to stories of great men in Denmark so that we become one with them."[22]

The Danish folk school, however, did not do as well in Michigan as its counterpart did in Iowa. First- and second-generation Danes were recruited by Lutheran pastors, but growth was limited, and enrollment remained low. By the school's second year there were twenty-one students at the school, many of whom came from the Trufant and Gowen areas in nearby Montcalm County, and in the years to come enrollment seldom exceeded forty students. The value of knowing Danish folklore and learning to read and write in Danish was lost on young adults, who saw little value in such knowledge in their new country. Furthermore, the private school tuition, which was fifteen dollars a month for girls and twenty dollars a month for boys,

*Ashland Folk High School operated in Grant, Michigan, between 1882 and 1938.
The first teacher was Kristian Ostergaard. Courtesy of the White Cloud Community
Library, White Cloud, Michigan.*

including lodging, must have been a consideration for some families, who also had access to tuition-free public schools.

The Ashland Folk High School struggled to survive. An enthusiastic minority kept the school going, but a lack of broad support hurt the institution. Grundtvigian apostles were frustrated by the lack of interest, and financial problems soon emerged. Discouraged by the lack of funding and interest, one of the school's leaders, J. J. Petersen, wrote a pamphlet encouraging Danes to consider Ashland. Reportedly, not a single copy sold. Frustrated, Petersen left the school in 1888 and moved to Tyler, Minnesota, where he founded another Danish folk school, called Danebod.

Petersen had recruited Kristian Ostergaard during his tenure, and in the wake of his departure Ostergaard took over the school. Ostergaard, a talented hymn writer, poet, and teacher, lasted only two and a half years in the leadership position. When he departed, he went back to Denmark and helped found another Danish folk school.

Ostergaard was replaced by Lorentz Henningsen in the 1890s. Henningsen studied art in Denmark and was well-known for his paintings, one of which was done for the local church in the Grant area. He continued the pattern, however, and like Petersen and Ostergaard before him left after a short stay. Devoted educators consistently became discouraged at the Ashland Folk High School.

Still, the school attracted and fostered community leaders. Jens Jorgensen was born in 1853, in Borre, Møn, Denmark. Soon after he immigrated to America in 1897 he began teaching Danish history at the Ashland Folk High School. Pastor Jorgensen also served parishes all over western Michigan. His efforts were appreciated not only by the students of the school but also by outsiders. King Christian X named Jorgensen a member of the Knights of the Order of the Dannebrog.

Ashland opened and closed several times between 1882 and 1938. One of the bright spots of this period was the construction of the school's gymnasium in 1888. Gymnastic competitions and celebrations helped make the gymnasium a community center for local Danes. Another highlight for the school was the annual Fourth of July celebration that drew as many as one thousand people.

Despite these contributions to the community, the school encountered major problems. In 1894 the Grundtvigians and the Inner Mission further divided over the issue of Americanization and integration. Danish folk schools, which encouraged Danish language and culture, became an ideological battleground. In 1903 the Michigan Danish Folk High School closed again and when the school building and gymnasium went unused, except for special occasions, for nearly a decade it appeared that the dream of a Grant area Danish folk school was dead. But in 1913, under the direction of Peter Rasmussen, the school reopened and witnessed a small revival. Rasmussen attracted new students to the school by offering novelty courses and by allowing both men and women to enroll during the winter semester, where only male students had wintered over in the past.[23] Danes from Montcalm County were recruited and for seven years the school kept its doors open, thanks in large part to Rasmussen's willingness to accept a small salary.

Despite his relative success, and like his predecessors, Rasmussen moved on to another Danish folk school when he left the school in 1920. He accomplished his dream of setting up a Danish school in Alberta, Canada, when the Dalum Folk School opened in 1921. After Rasmussen left, the Grant area school closed. Chester A. Graham, who then worked as a resident director at the school, attributed the closure to more than just Rasmussen's departure.

Students at the Ashland Folk High School, Grant, Michigan. Courtesy of the White Cloud Community Library, White Cloud, Michigan.

In Graham's words "intense anti-foreigner hysteria," triggered by World War I, hurt the school.[24]

In 1928, a new group of educators became interested in reopening the school. Though the Danish flavor and nature remained, the school opened under the new name American Folk School. At this point, the school was a progressive place where "teachers were students and students were teachers." Without degree requirements or hard deadlines, students conversed on a wide range of topics. Husbands and wives attended the school together and took advantage of the marriage classes. Like the Danish Folk High School before it, the American Folk School served as an institution for living, not just learning. People from all over America came to the school to attend the summer sessions. This final incarnation of the school stayed open with low enrollment until 1938.

In countless Michigan communities, far removed from Ashland Folk High School, Danish children attended the local public schools. The desire to teach the Danish language and culture, nevertheless, remained strong. For example, Maren Nielsen in Menominee County taught her children Danish around the dining room table. Some families sent their children to Danish summer church camps to encourage the cultivation of their culture.

The Danish Folk High School helped build a more vibrant Danish culture and community in Montcalm County. Danes here were often farmers, like Rasmus Hansen, who immigrated to Ashland in 1900. Hansen purchased a farm and became one of the first alfalfa farmers in the area. Other Danish farmers left Iowa for Ashland, where they could afford more land. Other Montcalm area Danes owned small businesses; Christen Osterby, who immigrated to Grant in 1915, owned a well-known bakery. A Danish Evangelical Lutheran Church was established in Grant to meet spiritual needs. It and the short-lived Danish folk school helped the Danish communities in Newaygo and Montcalm Counties establish and maintain a strong sense of identity.[25]

Danish Brotherhood

Whereas folk schools were established to teach young people of Danish descent in America what it meant to be Danish, fraternal organizations, such as the Danish Brotherhood, were founded to help first-generation immigrant Danes maintain their ethnic identity.[26] Nineteenth-century Danes were accustomed to living in tight-knit communities. The size and makeup of Denmark stood in stark contrast to Michigan; whereas Denmark's 16,576 square miles were considerably developed, Michigan's 58,216 square miles included vast areas of wilderness. Some organizations helped ease the transition from Denmark to Michigan by providing solidarity and forming strong ties with the homeland.

Many Danes settled in parts of Michigan where few spoke Danish. In these cases, Danish organizations and social clubs helped make up for the lack of the usual extensive safety net of friends and family. In an age before public assistance, ethnic social organizations provided death and burial policies and, later, financial assistance. The most prominent of these organizations was the Danish Brotherhood, followed by the Danish Sisterhood.

In the 1880s in Omaha, Nebraska, Mark Hansen started a branch of the Danish organization De Danske Vaabenbrødre, or, the Danish Brothers in Arms. Hansen, a veteran of the Danish army who also served in the American Civil War, sought to expand the Danish Brothers in Arms' benefits to other Danish immigrant men. In 1881, four other groups consolidated with Hansen's group to form the Danish Brotherhood. The first Brotherhood lodge in Michigan was Lodge No. 6 located in Negaunee, Michigan, in Marquette County.

*Danish Brotherhood members relaxing in the Danish Brotherhood hall. Courtesy
of the Mason County Historical Society at Historic White Pine Village, Ludington,
Michigan.*

The Brotherhood kept high ethical standards. Men were regularly refused membership or kicked out for immoral behavior. A blacklist served
as a national registry and ensured that no man was disallowed in one lodge
and then allowed in another, making the Brotherhood a relatively exclusive
organization.

Initially, the Brotherhood provided only survivor benefits and sickness
and death benefits for members and their families. At first, benefits were
minimal, but after years of shrewd management, enough funds were gathered to invest, and this allowed the organization a greater degree of liberty in
providing assistance. By 1902, $245,000 in insurance benefits had been paid
out, and the Brotherhood started to offer financial support to members who
were unemployed or experiencing other economic hardships.

The Brotherhood's membership grew quickly. At the end of 1882 the
Brotherhood included six lodges and roughly two hundred members. Ten
years later it boasted forty-one lodges and close to two thousand members.
In Michigan, the Negaunee lodge was followed by lodges in Manistee, Muskegon, Greenville, and Detroit, among others.

A typical Michigan Brotherhood lodge was established in Muskegon. Lodge number thirty was incorporated July 23, 1888. Members initially met in a Knights of Labor hall, but the lodge, led in part by Niels Nielsen and J. Rasmussen, eventually moved the meetings to the Scandinavian Hall. In typical Brotherhood style, the Muskegon Brotherhood not only provided benefits but also encouraged Danish culture, heritage, language, and pride. The initiations, camaraderie, and activities of the Muskegon Brotherhood created a deep bond. When a member died, two Danish Brotherhood members stood by the coffin for a night.

The Danish Brotherhood's reach extended over all of Michigan. From Detroit to Negaunee the Brotherhood was a focal point for many Danish men who incorporated the organization into their life as a part of what it meant to be Danish American. Membership slumped during the 1920s as immigration slowed and fewer Danes arrived in Michigan. It was also probably somewhat dampened by the fact that the Danish Lutheran Church sometimes opposed the Brotherhood because it was a secret society. Nevertheless, aggressive recruitment kept membership from completely dwindling, and in Michigan, the Brotherhood remained vibrant well into the twentieth century. At a convention held for the Brotherhood on September 16, 1963, in Pennsylvania, Viggo Mikkelsen, a member of the Detroit lodge, became the American president of the Danish Brotherhood.

One of the Danish Brotherhood's most notable Michigan members was George P. Everson. Everson, whose father was from Jutland, was born in Detroit in 1893 and joined the organization as a young man. He attended the University of Michigan and became successful in corporate America. Everson worked for forty years in the auto industry. He first worked for Maxwell Motors, which eventually became a part of the Chrysler Corporation. In 1939 he was appointed the Royal Danish vice-consul for Michigan. When Denmark was occupied by Nazi Germany in 1940 Everson organized the Danish Emergency Committee of Detroit to provide assistance. Everson's efforts earned him a medal for his service; the royal family and President Eisenhower acknowledged Everson's work. In many ways, Everson personified what the Danish Brotherhood stood for. He was a helping hand to the Danish, and he prided himself on his heritage and felt a special bond to his brethren. He was a model citizen in moral character and in civic virtue.

The friendships that the Danish Brotherhood provided strengthened ethnic bonds for Michigan's Danes. The Brotherhood helped Danes retain their culture and also provided practical benefits. In the age before health and life insurance the Danish Brotherhood filled the gap. By 1940 national membership was fifteen thousand.[27] While numbers have diminished, the Danish Brotherhood still exists today.

Danish Sisterhood

It was also important for Danish women to have their own ethnic social organizations. The Danish Sisterhood was born in Negaunee, Michigan, in Marquette County, in 1883.[28] Christine Hemmingsen, the wife of a Negaunee Danish Brotherhood Lodge No. 6 member, formally founded the Danish Sisterhood after a traumatic event. A friend of Christine's died, leaving behind a husband and children. Hemmingsen, who was familiar with the Brotherhood and its medical and death benefits, established the Sisterhood to help with funeral costs and expenses related to illness; in this way the Danish Sisterhood began as a medical and death benefits society.

Christine Hemmingsen was born January 30, 1840, in Orup, Denmark. She was wed in 1861 at the age of twenty-one to her husband Niels. In 1873 the couple decided to move to America. One Danish friend warned them that they should not be fooled by immigrants who made it sound like "in America cooked birds will fly into your mouth if you open it wide enough."[29] Despite his warnings, Christine and Niels left for America on August 1, 1873. After immigrating to America, settling in Negaunee, and founding the sisterhood, Christine served as the Danish Sisterhood's first president. Like the brotherhood, the sisterhood provided death benefits and had a code of conduct. The sisterhood also took on civic and charitable activities. During World War II, the sisterhood raised money to help Denmark. In 1930 there were approximately seven thousand members located in lodges throughout America.[30] Today, the sisterhood continues to raise money for scholarships.

Religion, education, and Danish social organizations were all structured institutions meant to bring Danes together. In the process these organizations promoted and maintained Danish culture. They served the desires of Michigan Danes by providing religious training, education, and friendships while adding a unique Danish flavor to daily life.

Table 1. Danes in Michigan, 1860–1920

	Counties with Populations of over 100 Danish Immigrants					
	1860	1870	1880	1900	1910	1920
MICHIGAN	86	778	3,862	3,620	3,769	4,352
Kent	7	33	179	251	244	207
Manistee	1	146	534	400	295	211
Marquette	1	74	281	139	116	78
Mason	2	6	267	217	230	236
Menominee	N/A	10	139	190	167	122
Montcalm	18	181	863	746	762	640
Muskegon	7	78	276	200	213	241
Newaygo	N/A	4	183	62	65	69
Wayne (Detroit)	16	21	96	161	294	1,088

Table 2. Danish Population in Michigan and the United States, 1850–1930

Census Year	Danes in Michigan	Danes in the U.S.	Largest Concentration
1850	13	1,838	New York: 429
1860	192	9,962	California: 1,392
			Utah Territory: 1,824
1870	1,354	24,574	Wisconsin: 5,212
			Utah Territory: 4,957
1880	3,513	53,499	Wisconsin: 8,797
			Utah Territory: 4,957
1890	6,335	132,543	Iowa: 15,519
1900	6,390	154,284	Iowa: 17,102
1910	6,315	181,649	Iowa: 17,961
1920	7,178	189,154	California: 18,721
1930	7,210	179,474	California: 23,175

Michigan's Danish Communities

Montcalm County Danes

The earliest known Michigan Danes arrived in the 1850s in Montcalm County.[31] Montcalm County offered the land, economic opportunity, and escape that many Danes were looking for. Located in western lower Michigan, northeast of Grand Rapids, Montcalm County was one of the many burgeoning settlements built on logging. White pines were logged from the dense surrounding forests, processed in the local saw mills built on the banks of the Flat River, and then shipped to eager markets. Though Denmark was not especially known for agriculture, Danes were hardly deterred. Greenville was adopted by Danish pioneers who commenced to build what became known as the Big Dane Settlement.

Christian Johnson, an adventurous Danish veteran, both directly and indirectly attracted many Danes to Greenville. Johnson was unsatisfied with life in Denmark, and particularly resented the privileges of the upper classes, of which he was not a part. After saving some money, Johnson left for America. He eventually settled in Montcalm County and sent enthusiastic letters home to Denmark in the mid-1850s. In one letter, Christian encouraged his brother Erastus to emigrate by emphasizing the economic opportunity, kind people, and beautiful women in Michigan. Johnson's letters encouraged limited Danish immigration to Greenville from the Sæby parish, on the island of Zealand.

August Rasmussen was one of the first Danes influenced by Johnson's optimistic letters. Rasmussen eagerly embraced Johnson's utopian views of America. In the last days of April 1856, Rasmussen, who like Johnson was a veteran, married Ane Fredrickson. Ane and August were in their midtwenties, without children, and eager to escape the economic conditions of Denmark and immigrate to the land of the "golden rocking chairs."[32]

On May 10, 1856, the Rasmussens departed from Denmark. Left behind were their closest friends and family members. They arrived in New York City on July 26, 1856. After nearly three more months of difficult travel by cart, horse, train, and ship, the Rasmussens arrived in Greenville with only "dust, dirt, [and] lice."[33] A satchel with the Rasmussens' prized Bible and hymnbook was stolen in New York; the delivery of other essential possessions was delayed after they were mistakenly shipped to Grandville.

Initially, August Rasmussen was unimpressed with Johnson's situation. Johnson lived in a modest dwelling and owned little land. Despite Johnson's economic struggles, Rasmussen saw potential in his new environment. Reflecting upon his experiences years later, Rasmussen reminisced that upon his arrival in Greenville, America seemed like a promised land. Most important, in Rasmussen's view, Michigan was not the land of aristocratic nobles.

Montcalm County provided ample opportunity for land ownership. In Denmark, even into the 1890s, most men of Rasmussen's status would've been fortunate to own a six- to eight-acre plot of land. This hardly compared to the eighty-acre tract of land that Rasmussen purchased in the 1850s for two dollars an acre.

August Rasmussen sent glowing letters to the Sæby parish. The year after the Rasmussens' arrival in 1856, thirty-six people from the Sæby parish left for Greenville. Rasmussen wrote:

> We can here get a good house to live, and all the stove wood we need free of charge. Here are thousands of acres of good farming land to be had almost for nothing. Here is more than enough land for all the people in the county where you live. Here are good and noble people. Think what a good opportunity you can secure for each of your children, while in Denmark they cannot get a poor shanty.[34]

The Sæby parish was home to a population of approximately 1,700, and most of the land belonged to a select few individuals. The social hierarchy, while not impossible to break through, was constraining. The king, nobility, squires, vicars, and civil servants formed the upper crust of society. The upper classes monopolized status and wealth.

In Montcalm County this was not the case. Danish immigrants found opportunity in the budding lumber industry where strong backs were needed more than a strong command of the English language. Working conditions were tough but for those willing to labor there was money to be made. Simultaneously, logging made farmland accessible, plentiful, and reasonably priced.

Danish men who came to the area often worked in the lumber industry during winter and as farmers or farmhands during warmer months. This allowed Danish immigrants to make money from logging while planting subsistence crops and raising milk cows. The women played an indispensable role in running the farms. Ane Rasmussen gathered berries for trade, sewed clothes, and likely cared for the cows. The butter and egg trade with local merchants was handled by women, making women an important part of the daily economy. Eventually cash crops overtook subsistence farming; potatoes became an important part of the Montcalm County economy.

As Montcalm County continued to prosper and grow, the nation drifted toward the Civil War. The Danes were mostly loyal to the Union and some joined the abolitionist cause. The founder of the Danish settlement, Christian Johnson, who gained military experience in the First Schleswig War against Prussia, enrolled his services with the Union. He died when a bullet struck him in the head in his first battle of the war. Later in the war Greenville Dane Peter Gooseman was captured and placed in the infamous Andersonville prison; he escaped, emaciated, after six months. A fellow Montcalm County Dane was not so lucky; Andersonville claimed his life.

After the Civil War Danish emigrants continued to find their way to Montcalm County. Danish emigration from 1860–1880 accelerated due to poverty within Denmark, which was caused by, among other issues, competition for land within a rapidly growing population. Another factor behind this wave of emigration was the military defeat Denmark suffered at the hands of Austria and Prussia in the 1860s. To escape service in the German military, and the suppression of Danish culture, many Danes left North Schleswig, an area between Denmark and Germany. Some Danes who arrived in Montcalm County were eluding conscription in the Prussian army.

The Danish were warmly received in Montcalm County. The county paper, the *Greenville Independent*, on May 8, 1870, excitedly announced the arrival of thirty more Danes and more on the way. On April 29, 1880, the *Greenville Independent* announced the arrival of fifty more Danes. The Danes built a vibrant ethnic culture; a church, a brotherhood lodge, and a Danish newspaper, *Dansk Folkeblad*, were established.[35]

Within a few decades after their arrival in Montcalm County in the 1850s, the massive forests of white pines were clear-cut and many Danes moved to the countryside to farm. Others took to white-collar jobs in the county like banking and law, and still others left Montcalm County and the Danish settlement altogether.

Soren Petersen was one Dane who found work in Montcalm County outside of the lumber industry. Originally from a small farm just a few miles outside of Copenhagen, Petersen won a lottery as a young man. He used his winnings to attend a top-notch dairy school, which was not surprising, as Denmark was experiencing an agricultural revolution and was a world leader in innovation for dairy production. In 1903, Petersen came to America to work in creameries. In 1911 he settled in Greenville, built his own creamery, and ran Petersen's City Creamery until 1927 when stiff competition forced him to close the business. After his creamery's closing, Petersen opened his own ice cream shop and in 1932 received the honor of placing fourth in an international cottage cheese contest.

Coming from a country that covers 16,600 square miles to Michigan, a state over three and a half times as large, meant that the web of Danish communities and culture was stretched incredibly thin. Compared to many other immigrant groups, Danes were few and far between. Montcalm County was one of Michigan's few exceptions. Greenville became a repository for Danish culture by attracting Danish immigrants from the Sæby parish in Zealand. In later decades Danes from other parts of Denmark arrived. With numerous Danes in the Greenville area, a Danish subculture emerged. Attempts to build Danish churches and schools were made and holidays and festivities from the Old Country were celebrated.

Today, Greenville continues to pay tribute to its Danish heritage. Since 1964 the city has hosted the Danish Festival, which attracts as many as eighty

Typical Danish immigrant farm in Dixon, a Kent County Community. Stena Ane Christine Petersen (born 1864) in the center. Courtesy of the Flat River Historical Society, Greenville, Michigan.

thousand people every year and includes selecting a Miss Danish Festival Queen. A drive in the countryside reveals many connections to Montcalm County's Danish immigrants. There are Danish cemeteries, roads with Danish names, and former Danish Lutheran churches. Reading the Danish tombstones in the cemeteries reveals an interesting sign of how the immigrants adjusted to their new home country in that some tombstones have inscriptions in both English and Danish.

Detroit Danes

Detroit's ideal location on the Great Lakes in the heart of the country allowed it to grow in the nineteenth century.[36] Although it attracted many immigrants due to its variety of industries, Danes generally were not attracted to the city because of their inclination toward farming. In 1860 there were only about two dozen Danes in Detroit. They were employed in trades such as brick and cabinet making, painting, general labor, shoemaking, and carpentry. There was even a sailor and a ship carpenter in the mix. Of the eighty-six Danes in Michigan, the largest number of them were either farmers in Montcalm and Oceana Counties or working in the woods of Muskegon County. This focus on rural settlement would continue until the post-World War I era when in 1920 Wayne County dominated the state in terms of economic prosperity with 1,088 Danes who, like thousands of others, were attracted to Metro Detroit because of the jobs available in the booming automobile industry and the glamour of urban life. This is exemplified by the Ford Motor Company. The Ford assembly line made mass production possible in numbers previously unimaginable. In just fifteen years, between 1904 and 1919, employment in Detroit's auto industry went from less than 3,000 to over 100,000. Many of these new employees were immigrants. Immigrants came from all corners of Europe, including Scandinavia. By 1925 immigrants made up an estimated 600,000 people, or almost half of the city. Detroit's large immigrant population helped make it one of the most dynamic cities in the world.

Detroit offered ample economic opportunities directly and indirectly linked with the auto plants. Danes sought this work and, like other immigrant groups, developed their own neighborhoods where their language and culture dominated. In Detroit the Danish neighborhood was centered at Twelfth Street and Forest Avenue, but Danes also built in the historic northwest part of the city. The main neighborhood was working class; it supported Danish stores, churches, social clubs, civic groups, brotherhoods, sisterhoods, a symphony orchestra, and business associations.

The Danes arrived in Detroit as early as 1853 and immigration to the area peaked around the 1920s. In 1880 there were an estimated seventy-one Danes living in the Detroit area and by 1951 Detroit had approximately 5,200 Danes. The large influx of Danes made it possible to start many different Danish societies and social clubs. A Danish bowling league, a national committee, a soldiers' association, and volunteer services all emerged to help the Danes in the Detroit area retain their ethnic identity. Danish newspapers were also popular among Detroit's Danes; the *Scandinavian Record, Danish Pioneer, Soldaten,* and *Norse Civic News* were all important avenues of information.[37] At the same time, Detroit's Danes embraced America. Detroit-area Dane Peter Lisberg—who was born in 1893 at Randers, Denmark, and came to America in 1915—was a member of the successful 1920 American Olympic team. The Olympics were held in Antwerp, Belgium, not far from the country Lisberg left just five years prior.[38]

In 1905 Detroit's Danes formed a lodge of the Danish Brotherhood and in 1916 they owned their own brotherhood hall. As immigration slowed and the Danish population aged a Danish retirement home became necessary. Fortunately, a Danish committee formed and a Danish memorial garden and retirement home was built with the intention of showing "appreciation for the efforts of early Danish immigrants."[39] The retirement home was built in 1948 and opened in 1949 in Rochester, Michigan, on former farmland. In 1962 Danes built a fountain garden at the retirement home. The home housed some Detroit Danes until it closed in 1977 after the State Health Department stated that "major changes had to take place."[40]

One of the most important organizations for Danes was the Fremad Society. The fraternal group was formed in Detroit around 1892. It gave Danes an opportunity to socialize and retain their Danish culture. Picnics, dances, socials, a church, and parades were all put together by the society. Fremad also operated as a beneficial organization for members in times of need. The Fremad Society continued to grow until the Great Depression, when membership fell from 300 to 125. Nevertheless, the group persisted in its mission to foster Danish culture while looking after fellow Danes, even if they weren't members. Detroit's poor and needy people of Danish descent were discouraged from reliance on public support because the society provided financial assistance.

Germany's invasion of Denmark in April of 1940 angered Detroit's Danes. The Fremad Society was especially active during World War II. They supported the Allied cause through the regular purchase of war bonds and paid the annual dues for members who joined the armed forces. Detroit Danish organizations united to raise funds for the underground movement in Denmark against Nazi Germany. In early 1945, the famed comedian, pianist, and critic of Nazism, Victor Borge, did a two-hour routine at the Danish Brotherhood's headquarters. The show raised money to support the Danish Emergency Committee of Detroit, which provided financial assistance to war-torn Denmark. Victor Borge went on to have an illustrious career in the United States that included appearances on *The Dean Martin Show* and *The Tonight Show Starring Johnny Carson*. Ove Rostgaard, a trustee of the Detroit Danish Brotherhood Lodge, claimed that he paid Borge, "the first money he made in the United States—$50 for a performance at our old hall."[41]

Music also united Detroit Danes, especially around the holidays. In the late nineteenth century Detroit's Danish organizations began to meet annually to celebrate Midsummer's Day on the Ann Arbor Trail. The celebration included games, Danish folk dancing, and singing. Danes also sang during the rest of the year in the Danish choir known as Bel Canto. Another group, the Danish Symphony Orchestra, began in 1929. The orchestra evolved into the Scandinavian Symphony Orchestra and claimed to be the sole ethnic organization of its kind in the Midwest. They made several performance trips to Europe.[42]

Detroit served as a hub of Danish activity in the Midwest. In 1931 the Danish Brotherhood celebrated its fiftieth anniversary in Detroit. The celebration was held at the Book-Cadillac Hotel with as many as eight thousand attendees. Both in peace and war time Danish women's organizations found valuable ways to contribute to the preservation of Danish culture while contributing to the Detroit community. Danish women's groups frequently centered on the church; for instance, in 1940 the Danish American Women's Volunteer Service, an important charitable organization, celebrated their first anniversary in St. Peter's Danish Evangelical Lutheran Church.

St. Peter's Danish Evangelical Lutheran Church was a significant part of the Danish community. The church was founded in 1882 when thirty-three of the seventy-one Detroit Danes united to create it. It was Detroit's eighth Lutheran congregation. By 1888 support for the church grew enough for the congregation to buy a church building on St. Catherine's Street. The congregation used the building until 1906. Some of the early pastors were Norwegian, thereby linking the Danes with the Norwegian Synod. In 1940, however, the church joined the Danish Synod. Later, this became the American Evangelical Lutheran Church before being combined with several other Lutheran bodies in 1962 to become the Lutheran Church in America.

In 1939 the Danish royal couple, Crown Prince Frederick and Princess Ingrid, made an appearance in Detroit. This delighted local Danes. The couple was greeted by an estimated 2,700 Danes in the Michigan Central Depot. A banquet was held for the couple at the Book-Cadillac on April 26th; the cost of attendance was $3.50 a plate. More than seven hundred people attended. The Danish Folk Dance Society, dressed in Icelandic and Danish costumes for the royal couple, ushered and performed at the banquet. During their stay in Detroit the couple met some of Detroit's most powerful businessmen. They were the guests of Henry Ford at a local auto plant and later visited with William S. Knudsen, the president of General Motors. Knudsen himself was a proud Dane.

William S. Knudsen made his way to Detroit after emigrating from Denmark around the turn of the century. He worked for the ship, bicycle, and railroad industries and then began working for the Ford Motor Company. His managerial prowess and engineering expertise allowed him to move up the ranks. In the 1930s Knudsen began to work in higher management for General Motors. He was promoted to the position of president of the company. During World War II Knudsen's skill and reputation attracted the attention of the federal government. Under President Franklin Delano Roosevelt, Knudsen was named "Lieutenant-General and top directive head of the industrial program in World War II." Another Dane followed a similar path to Knudsen; his name was Charles Sorensen, the man Henry Ford called "Cast-Iron Charlie."

Charles Sorensen was born September 7, 1881, in Copenhagen. His family and ancestors spent the previous two centuries working in parishes. This ended when Charles Sorensen's father, Søren Sørensen, immigrated to America in the 1880s. Søren had a strong interest in running. He was captivated by a world-famous Danish runner known as "Little Sorensen." He followed the runner's career with religious-like devotion and the two developed a special friendship. When Little Sorensen traveled to America and competed in races he sent letters back encouraging Søren to immigrate to America; Søren soon obliged.

Søren left for America without his wife and child. After a year and a half he found suitable work and sent for his family to join him. Charles and his mother left Denmark in the mid-1880s when Charles was four years old. They arrived in New York and then traveled to Pennsylvania where Charles and his mother reunited with Søren. By this time Søren worked as a draftsman. Their stay in Pennsylvania lasted only a few years until Little Sorensen, who had been bustling around the country winning running races, moved to Buffalo, New York. Søren followed what Charles called his father's "fleet-footed idol." The seemingly impulsive move to Buffalo proved to be economically beneficial. Søren rose in the ranks working for Jewett Stove Works and was promoted to the position of superintendent.

Buffalo was one of the hubs of bicycle racing and production at the time. This spurred the mind of the young Charles. At the time, some of the first motorcycles were used in Buffalo to help pace bike racers. Charles realized that if motorized vehicles were ever produced in great scales there would be ample opportunity for someone skilled in patternmaking. At the age of fourteen Charles gained valuable experience in auto part patternmaking working as an assistant to an architect-surveyor. His formal education began at sixteen when his work as an architect-surveyor's assistant and pattern-maker inspired him to enroll in night classes. The German instructor helped him gain a firm grasp on mathematics, something that became invaluable to Charles later in life.

At the age of sixteen or seventeen, during the Spanish-American War, the ambitious and patriotic Charles tried to enlist in the navy. The loss of two fingertips, however, excluded him from directly participating in the war effort. Instead, he went back to employment as a woodworking patternmaker.

Not long after Charles was rejected by the navy, his father left for Detroit. Charles followed. By then Charles's reputation was well established. Charles had previously worked as the temporary foreman of a pattern shop in Milwaukee, Wisconsin, and this sharpened his experience with auto part patternmaking. Once back in Michigan, Detroit provided Charles with additional opportunities. He took jobs delivering beer, working on cast iron, working as a patternmaker's apprentice, and even found employment as a traveling salesman selling gas and oil stoves. Charles's position working as a traveling salesman was a business failure but it did lead him to meet his future wife, Helen Mitchell, who married him two years after their initial meeting.

In Detroit Charles reconnected with a bicycle racing friend from Buffalo, Tommy Cooper. He introduced Charles to a man interested in having his ideas put into pattern form. His name was Henry Ford. From there a professional and personal relationship blossomed.

Sorensen started out by doing some side work for Ford. Ford was more known for his car racing than his mass-scale production at the time, but Charles's acquaintance with Ford soon evolved into a full-time job. His ability to work with castings helped Ford realize the dream of building a car for the masses and prompted Ford to give him the nickname "Cast-Iron Charlie." Charles continued to gain the respect of Ford, who trusted him to put his ideas into visible form. Ford, who lacked Charles's artistic skill, appreciated his handiwork.

Charles helped develop many of the things that are identified as quintessential Henry Ford. For instance, according to Charles, the highly coveted five-dollar-a-day pay at Ford Motor Company and the moving assembly line were both largely the products of his own efforts.[43]

Charles recounted that, "For about twenty years I was in complete charge of all Ford production."[44] His ability to astutely maneuver around Ford's idiosyncrasies and temperament benefited him. This made it possible for Charles to do something that many people could not do: get along with Henry Ford. Charles saw Ford as a transformational American hero. For Charles, Abraham Lincoln and Henry Ford were analogous.

In World War II Charles helped galvanize production of B-24 bombers for Allied forces. Charles brought assembly line efficiency to the construction of B-24s. As Charles put it, "instead of one B-24 a day by the prevailing method I saw the possibility of one B-24 an hour by mass production assembly lines." His role in helping lead Ford wartime productions was so important that he even had contact with the president of the United States in order to bridge communication gaps arising from personal conflict between Ford and Roosevelt.

The successes of Charles Sorensen and Knudsen were the things of Danish immigrant folklore. These were two Danish boys who, seemingly destined for a life of relative obscurity, were able to rise to the top of corporate America. Other Danes did well too. Detroit Danes worked as blacksmiths, craftsmen, and bakers, helping turn the Danish community in Detroit into a vibrant locale. For instance, Arthur Orum Taft, who was born in Aarhus, Denmark, in 1884, came to America in 1905 and worked as a successful blacksmith for the Ford Motor Company.

Muskegon Danes

Nineteenth-century immigrant Danes were often attracted to Michigan's coastal towns and cities.[45] In the 1850s logging settlements grew along the coast of Lake Michigan. These towns were frequently located next to rivers, placing them in perfect position to send lumber downstream to mills and across the lake to growing cities, such as Chicago. Business was lucrative. Three towns—Muskegon, Ludington, and Manistee—attracted Danes in search of jobs in the lumber industry.

Muskegon, located on the banks of the Muskegon River, proved an especially attractive settlement for Danes. The Danish found work in Muskegon's growing lumber industry and in other local industrial developments that made semi-skilled jobs available. The Danes, however, were not the first Scandinavians to arrive in Muskegon. In the 1840s the Norwegians arrived in Muskegon. Scandinavians, especially Danes, built houses on Kilgrubbins Hill and Peck and Delaware Streets. These two areas became known as the Danish neighborhoods. Scandinavian communities formed close bonds. For instance, Scandinavians celebrated traditional Scandinavian holidays and a Scandinavian lodge, known as Viking Lodge #57, had a popular midsummer festival every year.

One example of Scandinavian solidarity involves Chris Lahman, who was born in Denmark in 1845 and decided to emigrate at the age of twenty-three. In 1869 he went to Whitehall, just north of Muskegon, where he began working in the lumber industry. He continued working in the industry for the next several years. Later, in 1875, Lahman decided to become a grocer and business partner with a Norwegian man named Krogstad. Although Lahman eventually moved on and opened a saloon in the back of a railway depot (which was later destroyed by a fire), the two Scandinavian men worked together for six years.

Many activities and organizations existed for Muskegon's Danes. In 1874 a Danish church became available for locals. Danish Brotherhood Lodge No. 30 was incorporated in 1888 and a Danish Sisterhood lodge followed. The brotherhood was an important part of life for Danes in the area. The lodge celebrated its fiftieth anniversary in 1938; although as of this writing it is still in existence, there is no membership available.

Muskegon's Danes built a well-adjusted and vibrant community. The 1860s were a time of growth for Muskegon's Danes as the population climbed from five to fifty-two. Danes' low numbers made them blend into the broader Scandinavian society. They did well in this context and, when viable, broke off to form their own Danish social groups and celebrations.

Ludington Danes

North of Muskegon lies Ludington, Michigan.[46] Like Muskegon, Ludington was built on the shores of Lake Michigan and became home to a small settlement of Danes. The history of the Danes in Ludington parallels that of the Danish church built there in that both the town and the church grew

"Busy Big Store" Ludington, Michigan, circa 1898. Built in 1888 for Thomas P. McMaster as the "Big Store." Named "Busy Big Store" by N. P. Christensen in the 1890s. Courtesy of the Mason County Historical Society at Historic White Pine Village, Ludington, Michigan.

to be religious and cultural centers. Danes made the church the center of their life. At first, Scandinavians went to the same churches. But when the opportunity to build a Danish church in Ludington arrived, several Danes enthusiastically endorsed the idea. The church, which was constructed on South Madison Street, originated out of group meetings that began in 1878.

Nels Petersen was one of the earliest Danish arrivals. He began homesteading a farm in Victory Township in 1872. Like many Danish settlers, Petersen cleared his land for farming and worked in local industry. He cleared his land by piling the timber and burning it; one summer, the smoke was so bad that it was hard to breathe all season. Petersen also worked at a mill in Ludington approximately ten miles away. As a result, he frequently only spent the weekends at home with his family since the commute was too long to walk daily.

Danes came to Ludington, and the surrounding Victory Township, to work in a variety of trades. Some Danes owned shops and hardware stores, a few were butchers and grocers, and others worked in the dairy industry. A local shoe repair store was Danish-owned and there was even a Danish bakery and boarding house. Dane Nels P. Christensen owned the retail outlet the Busy Big Store and then went on to run a funeral home.

Danes also served in political office. Over the years a number of Danes and Danish Americans successfully ran for political office on the county and city level. Danish-born Peter Madison was mayor of Ludington from 1917 to 1922. Between 1964 and 1971 Hans Rasmussen served as a state representative from Ludington. Marjorie Jean Anderson, daughter of Danish immigrants, married Robert Griffin. He went on to be elected to both houses of Congress between 1957 and 1979 and served on the Michigan Supreme Court. As the wife of this noted Republican congressman, Marjorie played an important role actively supporting her husband's numerous political achievements at the state and national level. She and her husband were part of the first congressional group to go to China after President Nixon's initial trip. At Central Michigan University the Griffins' service was recognized by the es-tablishment of the Robert and Marjorie Griffin Endowed Chair in American Government.[47]

Ludington's Danish church held onto the native language for decades. By 1957, however, Danish was seldom used in church services, despite the attempts of congregation members to preserve their Danish culture through a variety of social activities such as the creation of cookbooks. The church became known as Victory Trinity Lutheran Church and joined the Evangeli-cal Church of America.

Manistee Danes

North of Ludington, along the coast of Lake Michigan, is Manistee, Michi-gan.[48] Settlers came to the area as early as 1827. The logging industry grew and a sawmill was constructed in 1841. Large ships soon arrived dropping off and picking up valuable timber cargo and supplies for the town.

In 1860 Jørgen Mortensen arrived in Manistee, making him the first Dane to settle in the area. Mortensen, who came from the Danish island of Falster, ran Manistee's first Danish boarding house. The Danish population grew and prospered until 1871 when a fire swept through the city. On October 8, 1871, the same day as the Great Chicago Fire, Manistee burned and approximately

Lake View House operated by Rasmus Rasmussen. Section at right built in 1876, section at left built by 1888 and still standing in 1979 at the northeast corner of Madison Street and 6th Street. Courtesy of the Mason County Historical Society at Historic White Pine Village, Ludington, Michigan.

half of the buildings were damaged or destroyed. Along with the rest of the community, the Danes fought the fire the best they could and collaborated as a Danish community to save valuables. Men worked tirelessly to bury goods and collect water to douse the flames while many of the women and children took boats out on the water to escape the fire. Some Danes believed that the end of the world was at hand.[49] Some Danish dwellings were rescued from the flames, but some Danes lost their homes and most of their possessions.

The fire burned one Danish boarding house, which increased demand for the two remaining. Fortunately, Mathies Peterson's boarding house held thirty to forty people and Lintrup Petersen's boarding house held around fifty, so between the two they were able to host the majority of the Danes who had been residing in the boarding house that burned. These Danish boarding houses were not country clubs. A local pastor who visited Petersen's boarding house described it as a "rough place."[50] New immigrants, vagabonds, and drunks were typical boarding house guests.

Drunkenness was a major problem in Michigan's logging settlements, and Manistee was no exception. In Manistee this resulted in extreme tension in the late nineteenth century when an estimated two thousand people signed a pledge for temperance, i.e., the restriction or banishment of liquor. Those who refused to sign the pledge fiercely protested the temperance movement. Protests against temperance led to the killing of horses and threats against life and property. Danes were not immune to the controversy.

One colorful Danish couple, Jorgen and Cecilia Sorensen, owned a saloon. At times the couple was at odds with local authorities. Nevertheless, even after their house burned down in 1872 they stayed in business. Jorgen ran the Scandinavian Workers' Society and the couple operated the Copenhagen Hotel; it became one of the area's primary Danish locales. The Scandinavian Workers' Society was important because it helped to alleviate the abuse local industry doled out to its workers. For example, employers paid their workers in script known by local residents as "Manistee money." While many in the community refrained from accepting this script or cheated immigrants of its value, Danish boarding houses and social and religious organizations accepted the script, which aided the workers by giving them other outlets for this questionable currency.

In Manistee, as in Ludington, Danes first attended the same churches as other Scandinavians but disagreements among the nationalities resulted in separate congregations. The Danes split off in the mid-1870s and formed their own church, Our Saviour's Lutheran Church. The church served as a repository for Danish language and culture and helped galvanize the temperance movement. Parishioners added a Danish-fashioned altar and wood carvings. The church, which still stands, is the nation's oldest standing Danish Evangelical Lutheran church.[51]

While the Danish church prospered so did local Danes. Ernest N. Salling and Rasmus Hansen founded a large lumber business and Salling rose in the ranks of the church hierarchy. Nels Johnson was one of the most successful Danes in Manistee. Johnson was born November 26, 1838, in Skaftelev, Denmark, to a blue-collar family. The oldest of six siblings, Johnson began work at the age of seven by taking care of sheep, geese, and cattle. He worked hard and desired adventure, travel, and luxury; for instance, he dreamed of having a "hand organ and a monkey."[52] Later, Johnson tried to join the military as a drummer boy or trumpeter. When this failed he pursued several odd jobs: he delivered beer; worked at the famed amusement park, Tivoli; and eventually found work doing road construction as a teenager. Six years of working with heavy tools and fourteen-hour shifts exhausted Johnson.

In 1861 the military called Johnson up for training. Two years later, to avoid military service, Johnson left Hamburg for Liverpool. Without a passport, Johnson was nervous about being apprehended by the authorities. He eluded conscription by pretending to be a shepherd; he cleverly accompanied a flock of sheep onto a ship to escape notice. Once aboard he met other Danes immigrating to America and decided to join them and four hundred Irish immigrants on their voyage to Québec. Johnson was unable to pay his fare and relied on the generosity of a fellow Dane who loaned Johnson the money.

Johnson arrived in Québec unable to speak English. He managed to find his way to Milwaukee, Wisconsin, where he quickly found work. He earned a dollar a day working for two years in a blacksmith shop. Johnson worked his way up and began to earn more income, which afforded him the opportunity to start his own machine shop. In 1871, Johnson moved to Manistee where he believed there was greater opportunity for him. Regrettably, 1871 was the same year as the great fire. Johnson was uninsured and lost thousands of dollars' worth of valuables and tools.

Nels Johnson persisted notwithstanding the ill-fated turn of events. In 1872 Johnson entered into a partnership and worked diligently over the course of the next decade to turn his struggling machine shop into a healthy business. In 1895 he sold his part of the shop to his son and began focusing on building clock towers.

Johnson learned astronomical principles and other clock-related expertise through members of the faculty at the University of Michigan. He gained a reputation of constructing clocks that would last 100 years. He was also a successful machinist and toolmaker. At the height of Johnson's fame his clocks were sold worldwide—in China, England, India, and all over the United States.

Johnson's immigration experience was characteristic of Michigan's Danish immigrants. His motive for immigrating—to flee conscription—was typical of the period. Furthermore, Johnson's reliance on the generosity of other Danes to cross the Atlantic and get his feet on the ground was common. Lastly, Johnson's success as a businessman and a world-famous clockmaker fits with the theme of the relative success of Michigan's Danish immigrants.

In Manistee and throughout Michigan, whether in the lumber industry, auto industry, or even the clock industry, many Danes succeeded and rose to the top of their respective trades. In 1890 there were 778 Danes in Manistee County. Some of these Danes were successful entrepreneurs; the largest fish shop and saddle factory were owned by Danes. The most successful ice merchant in the area was also a Dane. The west coast of lower Michigan, with its abundant lumber resources, trade, and industrialization, provided Danes with the opportunities for success.

Menominee Danes

Menominee, Michigan, is located on the southwestern shore of Michigan's Upper Peninsula.[53] Danes arrived in significant numbers during the nineteenth century. Individuals came to the area for prospecting and homesteading as American territorial acquisitions attracted pioneers. As the nineteenth century progressed the demand for lumber rose and Menominee's economy and population grew. Like Muskegon, Ludington, and Manistee, Menominee was a logging town. The rich surrounding forests and Lake Michigan's proximity made it possible to efficiently and profitably ship lumber.

Menominee's factories and woods provided Danes with a variety of jobs and a vibrant Danish community emerged. A Danish Evangelical church, a summer school for Danish children, and Danish boarding houses helped attract and retain Danes.

The Nielsens were one notable local Danish family. Knud Nielsen was born August 7, 1866, in Herberg, a small village in Jutland near Videbæk. Nielsen's life in Denmark was not easy. Shortly after Knud's birth his father died from exposure and other complications emerging from service in the war with Prussia in 1864. Knud, his siblings, and his mother were devastated by the death. Knud's mother, Margareth I. Herborg, raised Knud and his siblings the best she could; nevertheless, the children were subjected to poverty-like conditions. Knud and his siblings were forced to take on responsibilities years beyond their age. At the age of six Knud began earning his way by herding sheep; his pay was food and tattered clothing. As a teen, Knud went to work on a farm near Herning. At the farm he met a young girl named Maren and the two became close friends.

Knud received little formal schooling. Despite this, his ingenuity and curiosity were present from a young age. Combining his intelligence with his boyish humor, he once designed a kite and attached it to a barrel; the kite pulled the barrel across fields, frightening local cattle.

Knud immigrated to America at the age of twenty-two. He arrived in New York broke and reliant on the generosity of Danish friends. He soon moved west to Menominee, Michigan. His letters to friends in Denmark reveal that Knud immigrated because of economic reasons. Nielsen went to work in the logging industry while he took up residence in a boarding house run by Anders and Marie, a Scandinavian couple.

Menominee's Danish community helped Knud transition to the American life. On September 17, 1892, Knud Nielsen joined the Menominee Lodge of the Danish Brotherhood. Knud took out a $1,000 policy with the brotherhood with a $1.11 premium; who the policy was for is unclear. It was either for his future wife, Maren, who he married over ten years later, or a female family member or friend with the same last name as him. Knud's chapter of the brotherhood, with its ninety-six members by 1896, provided him with Danish culture and friendships.[54]

Outside of the brotherhood Knud worked as a carpenter and a woodsman. While working in the woods, he sometimes found time to attend school during the winter and paid for tuition by firing the stove and cleaning the school. He traveled to work in lumber camps in other areas of northern Michigan and Wisconsin. During the Panic of 1893 Knud found work on the West Coast but he soon returned to Menominee.

During his time in Michigan Knud continued to write letters to his childhood friend Maren. Despite a decade of separation and a significant age difference, Knud confessed his love for Maren and the two sent friendly and romantic letters. Knud promised to return to Denmark and marry Maren. As early as 1897, five years before they were married, Knud referred to Maren as his bride.[55] The correspondence carried on for over a decade and culminated in Knud's return to Denmark, where the couple was married. Knud was prepared to settle with his new wife in Denmark but he soon realized that he despised Denmark's agricultural society. In 1902, the same year of their marriage, the couple left Denmark for Menominee, Michigan.

In Michigan, Danish women were few. Approximately sixty percent of Michigan's Danish immigrants were men, and many women who came to Michigan were married. Danish immigration to America also affected the male-female ratio in Denmark, where there was a surplus of single women for decades. For many, it was considered ideal to marry someone from the same ethnic background. This may help explain Knud and Maren's willingness to wait years and endure thousands of miles of separation.[56]

Maren adjusted well to life in Menominee. She was an active church member and coordinated many church and social activities. Knud, on the other hand, attended church less than Maren despite the fact that his brother Nils, who immigrated in the early 1890s, was an ordained minister who worked with the Cherokees of Oklahoma.

Politically, Knud leaned toward socialism; in one of his letters to Maren he described himself as "no friend of militarism."[57] Knud's confession, however, contrasted with some of his other letters. He wrote of the barbarity of the enemy during the Spanish-American War and indicated that he believed America to be righteously involved.

As a hobby, Knud built model steam engines, electrical generators, and other oddities. His ingenuity manifested itself in the invention of one of the earliest oscillating electric fans. Knud worked for local industry and his intellect and work ethic endeared him to management. At one point he was offered a management position. The socialist Knud rejected the offer on the grounds that he wanted to stand by his fellow laborers and not on the side of management.

Knud and Maren had two sons. They were intelligent boys raised in Danish customs. For instance, at Christmas, rice porridge with an almond was served and the family danced around the spruce tree and sang Danish songs. Their first child, Harald, was born on January 25, 1903, and by the age of three Harald was reading Danish. Maren used cookies as incentives to learn the language. Denmark was so important to the Nielsens that at the age of five Harald entered school speaking mostly Danish. Harald was an introverted child who showed a propensity for academics at a young age. Unlike his classmates, Harald preferred academics to sports. He took voice lessons, piano lessons, and possessed a great interest in theater. His younger and more extroverted brother, Alvin, also enjoyed school. Both brothers read Danish and excelled academically. They also fully absorbed the Danish heritage of their parents, who took in Danish immigrants.

Harald's academic promise and sense of Danishness were strengthened by the opportunities for Danish people in the area. A Danish summer school gave young Danes a place to learn about their Lutheran religion and Danish history and literature. Danish camps even brought in Danish American intellectuals. Harald graduated high school the third highest in a class of eighty-eight. With his giftedness, his zealously religious mother encouraged her son to become a clergyman. Harald obliged and enrolled in Grand View College in Des Moines, Iowa, a thoroughly Danish school. But Harald found the school to be less than he expected and he moved on. He decided to attend St. Olaf College in Minnesota; however, once again he was less than pleased. Finally he went to the University of Michigan in Ann Arbor and found himself in the academic environment he sought. He appreciated the large school's academic rigors. On June 17, 1929, Harald received a doctor of philosophy degree from the University of Michigan and that same year applied for and received a fellowship from the American-Scandinavian Foundation to study in Denmark. Later in the year he sailed for Denmark and on his arrival had the exhilarating experience of finally hearing everyone around him speaking Danish.

Harald soon returned to America, where he took a position at Ohio State University. He worked there for forty-one years, teaching physics and becoming chair of the department, and gained many accolades. He participated in the first cultural exchange program with the Soviet Union in 1958 and received a grant to study with renowned physicist Niels Bohr.[58]

Harald's younger brother achieved similar success. Taking his brother's cue, Alvin also attended the University of Michigan, where he received a doctorate in physics. In 1935 he began to teach physics at the University of Tennessee and during World War II Alvin helped the army study infrared spectroscopy in detection work.

Other Danes thrived as well. R. P. Sorenson, who came to America in 1877 at about the age of eleven, became a main owner of a well-established meat company, Sorenson & Wheaton. Danes also seized opportunities in Escanaba, in Delta County northeast of Menominee. One of the most interesting Danish entrepreneurs was Gus Asp, the father of Escanaba saloon keeper Charles Asp. Gus Asp's cigar and newspaper store was an Escanaba institution. His carefully made sign flashed back and forth, "Just Ask" "Gus Asp" and has become a historic landmark in downtown Escanaba.

Peter Jensen: Prominent Escanaba Citizen

Danish-born Peter Jensen was a state representative from Delta County serving five terms in office (1909–1910, 1911–1912, 1913–1914, 1919–1920, 1921–1922) and an Escanaba businessman. He was born of Danish parents on November 14, 1863, in the province of Schleswig, Denmark. Jensen was educated in the public schools and came to the United States at eighteen years of age. Living in Escanaba by 1893, he was engaged in the fish business under the firm name of Hansen & Jensen, which continued its business into the 1930s. In 1913 he branched out and became involved in the oil business with the coming of automobiles and eventually he was listed as a gas station proprietor. He married Jennie, a Danish immigrant, in 1905, and the two of them worked closely in their businesses. Jensen was a member of a number of fraternal lodges and in addition to being state representative he served for four years on the Escanaba City Council and held the office of township road commissioner. He is a fine example of many immigrants who successfully engaged in local and state government.

Stephenson Danes

Between 1875 and 1910 Stephenson, in the northern part of Menominee County, attracted Danes searching for work.[59] The lumber industry was one reason Danes chose Stephenson. Many Danes emigrated to escape Denmark's meager prospects for land ownership. Danes in the Stephenson area, however, were not purely motivated by economic factors—some left behind comfortable living conditions in Denmark to seek adventure.

Two Danish pioneers to Stephenson were Hans and Ane Marie Jorgensen; they arrived around 1875. The Jorgensens became a point of reference for other Danish immigrants. They built a log home and later extended it, making it possible for new immigrants from Denmark to be comfortably accommodated when they arrived.

Many of Stephenson's Danes first arrived in New York and then took the train to Stephenson. Upon arrival they were greeted by their Danish forerunners before eagerly seeking work in the lumber camps. Some Danes earned enough to purchase large tracts of land, such as Thomas Frederickson. Frederickson worked hard and became financially secure. He used his security to aid other Danes who immigrated to the area. One Danish youth recalled that Frederickson and his wife fed and looked after new Danish immigrants who had nowhere to turn. Frederickson's actions helped contribute to the strength of the Danish communal spirit. Families of Danes turned out for barn raising parties, occasionally canceled one another's debts, and gathered for social occasions.

Danish community spirit included religious devotion. When Stephenson Danes wanted to build a Lutheran Church around 1900, they worked together. One Danish family donated the lot for the construction of the church and other Danes, building their own homes at the time, donated one long for every nine the church paid for to help with the construction. After several years of dedication to the project the efforts paid off. The church, St. Johannes Danish Evangelical Church, was frequently led by pastors recruited from Menominee; Danish Brotherhood members took an active role in the church as well.

The church, christened in 1906, was short-lived. After World War I the Danish community dwindled as the younger generation became Americanized. This and the Spanish flu pandemic in 1918 that claimed the lives of healthy young Danes proved devastating for the church. The church slowly died and from 1929–1932, the building was almost abandoned. The church's end came when a lack of financial support forced the church to make the difficult decision to sell the building to a Mr. Plutchak, who purchased and disassembled the building for scrap.

Some Stephenson Danes kept close contact with friends and family in Denmark. Friendly letters to the Old Country shared their life in America. Kristine Henriksen's mother, Marie Mouritsen, corresponded with friends in Denmark in the late 1880s. The letters covered a variety of topics including deep religious convictions that many Danish pioneers held.

The Danes in Stephenson resembled Danes in many other areas in Michigan. They were involved in lumbering and farming and were strong supporters of the local Danish church as well as Danish fraternal organizations such as the Danish Brotherhood.

Marquette County Danes

The Marquette area, with its proximity to Lake Superior, mineral deposits, and rich forests, attracted many immigrants in the late nineteenth century.[60] Danes came to the area in search of work in the lumber industry and mines. They often worked these jobs for many years before retiring or transitioning to less back-breaking employment.

In 1880 there were 281 Danes living in Marquette County with the largest number residing in the iron mining districts of Ishpeming and Negaunee. It should be remembered that although Danes were one of the smallest groups of immigrants who settled in Michigan, in Marquette County they were surrounded by Norwegians (566) and Swedes (2,105) whose cultures and languages were similar. As a result this smaller group was not alone in the county.

Although there were a few Danes in the city of Marquette—where many of them were employed on the coal dock and a few were farmers in Chocolay Township to the south—the vast majority were located in the interior of the county. Most of them were miners or engaged in some occupation connected with mining—teamster, stonemason, blacksmith, laborer. A smaller number were employed in such positions as saloon keeper, bartender, plasterer, peddler, painter, and hostler. There was also a scattering of Danish immigrants who joined the professional ranks. For example, thirty-four-year-old Nels Hermingsen, residing with his Danish-born wife and children in Negaunee, was a veterinary surgeon. He and his wife moved to Michigan in 1875. James Hanson was an engineer and John Hanson (unrelated) was a justice of the peace.

From information gathered from historical records, it seems Danish families in the area usually did not turn their homes into boarding houses. However, the Christensen family in Negaunee was an exception. Hans, the head of the household, worked as a miner while his wife, Ann, and a servant girl, Mary Rasmussen, tended their ten-year-old son Anders and maintained the boarding house. There were eight Danish miners who boarded with the family and were provided with a bed used on a revolving basis, food, and clean clothes. It must be remembered that the miners' clothes usually were embedded with red iron dust and were difficult to wash clean by hand. However, the rent from the boarders usually matched the money made by Hans or any other household head working in the mines.

At this time most of the Danish women listed in the census were married and listed as "keeping house." Some widows made money by taking in boarders or were seamstresses. A few of the unmarried women in their twenties listed in the census were employed as domestic servants. Many of these women found the Danish Sisterhood, established in Negaunee in 1883, to be a source of comfort and connection with other Danish-born women. This situation was common throughout the state and continued over the years that followed.

In Negaunee, just outside of Marquette, Danish Brotherhood Lodge No. 6 was founded in 1882. President Henry Rasmussen, vice president Joseph Petersen, and a handful of other dedicated Danes took leadership roles in the early years of the organization. The Danish Brotherhood of the Negaunee area became an important part of the Danish experience in the following years. By December 1907, 138 members belonged to the Negaunee Lodge. The Danish Brotherhood of Negaunee provided the inspiration that led to the development of the Danish Sisterhood on November 21, 1883. This stands as the most unique contribution of the Marquette County Danes.

After 1900 Danish immigration to the area slowed, but Danish culture persisted. Not having a large enough population for their own ethnic church, many Danes attended the Norwegian Evangelical Lutheran Church in Ishpeming. However, parents gave history and language lessons to their children, celebrated Danish holidays and traditions, and shared favorite Danish recipes.

Thorvald M. Sorensen was one of the most interesting Danes in Marquette County. Sorensen set up a greenhouse on Washington and Third Street, close to the center of Marquette. He built an impressive greenhouse with roughly 12,000 square feet of glass. The greenhouse utilized steam heat. Like many Danes in and around Marquette, Thorvald Sorensen was a successful entrepreneur.

Another well-known Dane in Marquette County was Henry Rasmussen, an early pioneer settler in Negaunee and one of the founders of the Danish Brotherhood Lodge No. 6. Born in Lolland, Denmark, on February 18, 1850, at the age of twenty-two Rasmussen sailed for the United States and made his way to Negaunee where he worked as an engineer at the Jackson Mine until his retirement. Both Rasmussen and Sorensen exemplified the success many Danes achieved throughout Michigan.

The James and Emma Christesen family, circa 1890. James was born August 8, 1855, in Soro, Denmark. When he was age seven his parents immigrated to Wisconsin. James, his wife Emma, and their descendants lived and prospered in the border communities of the Upper Peninsula and northeastern Wisconsin. Courtesy of Russell Christesen and Carol Meyer.

Thoroughly Americanized sons (standing: Archie, Ellis, John; kneeling: Jesse, Ode, and Herbie) born to Danish immigrants James and Emma Christesen from Soro, Denmark. Photo taken in front of 1920s automobiles during holiday in the Upper Peninsula. Courtesy of Russell Christesen and Carol Meyer.

Conclusion

In reviewing U.S. census data approaching the mid-twentieth century in 1940, there were 107,982 Danes in the United States. Of that number 5,441 were residing in Michigan, with 3,402 living in urban settings, 1,204 living on farms, and 835 living in non-farm communities. It is interesting to note that forty years earlier the vast majority of Michigan Danes were living in rural areas. By the 1950 census the number of Danish immigrants in Michigan had dropped to 4,219 and twenty years later it had fallen to 2,379. This halving of the number of immigrants continued so that by 1990 there were 775 in the state. In 2000 1,430,897 people in the United States reported having Danish ancestry. The major factor for the decline in immigration to the United States by Danes was the improved economic conditions in Denmark after World War II.

Today over 50,000 Michiganders claim Danish ancestry. Michigan's Danish immigrants were a small but significant ethnic group. Danes were leaders in the auto industry, as seen in Detroit. They were inventive entrepreneurs, professionals, and even academics, as was the case in Manistee and Menominee. In general, Michigan's Danish immigrants fared well.

From their arrival the Danes began the process of assimilating into American society. By the 1930s the Danish language was rarely heard in church services. Nevertheless, despite slowing immigration to Michigan,

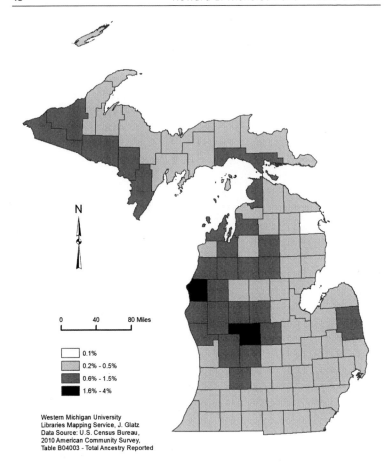

Distribution of Michigan's population reporting Danish ancestry (2010).

local Danes kept their culture alive.[61] Danish religion, education, and social organizations played an important part in the lives of Michigan's Danish immigrants. Even though the Danes were less than one percent of Michigan's population in 1940, they added to Michigan's rich ethnic diversity. They were proud of their Danish heritage and proud to be Americans.

Icelanders in Michigan

Russell M. Magnaghi

Introduction

Given the fact that Iceland is a small island nation with a miniscule population, immigration from the island was insignificant. Icelanders migrated to Wisconsin, Minnesota, and the Canadian province of Manitoba. Michigan seems to have been a point of transit on their travels west and as a result the Icelandic population of Michigan has been negligible. Further complicating identifying Icelanders is the fact that during the nineteenth century Iceland was a part of the Kingdom of Denmark. As a result United States census takers did not officially identify Iceland as a place of birth on their enumeration lists until the 1930 census. So we must make do with the information that we have for Icelandic immigrants.

The Island Nation

After Britain, Iceland is the second largest island in Europe—39,709 square miles—and the westernmost nation in Europe. It is located some 600 miles to the west of Norway and about 160 miles southeast of Greenland. Located barely to the south of the Arctic Circle, it has a mild and humid climate, especially along the southern and western coasts, which is influenced by the warm waters of the Gulf Stream and prevailing southwesterly winds off the Atlantic Ocean. Iceland's winters are warmer than those of New York, Zurich, and Michigan. It is an environment of ice and fire influenced by glaciers, hot springs (whose waters are used for heating), geysers, about 150 active volcanoes, icecaps, tundra, snow-capped peaks, vast lava deserts, and waterfalls. Parts of the coast are cut by fjords. Approximately 21 percent of the land lying near the coast is habitable and arable and used for grazing and farming. The capital and home to most of the nation's population is Reykjavík (Smoky Bay), named for the smoke from thermal springs.

Iceland was possibly the Ultima Thule, a term used by ancient writers to describe the little known region in the far north. It was visited by Irish monks who were fascinated by its monastic setting. Norse settlers fleeing Norwegian tyranny settled in western Iceland between 850 and 875 and brought along their Scottish and Irish slaves. Farming quickly became a way of life for these people. In 930 a general assembly, the Alþing, was established to govern the country and seventy years later Christianity was introduced, although paganism continued for a while afterward. Many of these events are preserved in the literature or sagas of thirteenth-century Iceland where Old Norse literature reached its greatest flowering.

Politically Iceland was a feudal state in which rival chieftains conducted bloody civil wars. This violence attracted Norwegian intervention, prompted by Snorri Sturleson. Snorri was a wealthy chieftain, historian, and probably the leading figure in medieval literature in the twelfth century. He tried to work with Norwegian King Haakon IV to attach Iceland to Norway. Due to inheritance questions and political intrigue Snorri was killed by a relative. Haakon finally incorporated Iceland into the archdiocese of Trondheim and in 1261–1264 obtained acknowledgment of his suzerainty by the Icelanders. Norwegian rule brought higher taxes and order with an imposed judicial system.

Iceland continued to be governed by Norway until 1380 when with the death of Olav IV the last of the Norwegian royal male line was extinguished and Norway and thus Iceland became part of the Kalmar Union, which included Sweden and Denmark. The Danes did not need Icelandic fish or homespun wool and as a result there was a substantial decline in trade with Iceland. During the Reformation of the early sixteenth century, Lutheranism was introduced. The seventeenth and eighteenth centuries saw Iceland plagued by pirate raiders from the south and Denmark imposed a trade monopoly, which was detrimental to the economy of the island and only ended

Mt. Hekla

Located in southern Iceland, Mt. Hekla (4,892 feet) has been one of Iceland's more active volcanoes, erupting some twenty times since 874. During the Middle Ages this active volcano was given the religiously inspired title "Gateway to Hell." One Cistercian monk wrote a poem claiming that the volcano was "the prison of Judas." As a result, by the nineteenth century this volcano was well-known throughout the world.

Mining companies are named randomly as was the Hecla Mining Company in 1866, several years after Mt. Hekla had an eruption. This company merged in 1871 and became the Calumet and Hecla Mining Company, one of the major copper mining companies in Michigan, and was known throughout the mining world as one of the most efficient and prosperous mines in the world.

in 1854. Volcanic eruptions and epidemics over the years caused further problems for the population.

In the nineteenth century there was a rebirth of national culture and there was a slow political development and reorganization. However it was not until 1918 that Iceland was declared a sovereign state in "personal union" with the Danish crown. During World War II, with the German occupation of Denmark, first the British and then the Americans occupied Iceland to halt German westward expansion. In 1944 Iceland gained its complete independence.

The population of Iceland in 2009 was 319,062. Sixty-four percent of the population lives in the greater Reykjavík area while the rest of the population lives in small communities throughout the country. About 25,000 Icelanders live on farms.

Earliest Immigration

The first Icelandic immigrants moved westward around the year 1000. In that year Leif Ericsson, who was born in Iceland, sailed to Greenland after a legal problem in Iceland and began a settlement. The cattle and dairy farms, religious establishments, and communities lasted for 500 years.

According to Viking lore, in 1004 Gudrid Thorbjarnardottir and Thorfinn Karlsefni led a party to North America following Leif Ericsson's voyages there. The group sailed in three boats containing sixty to seventy colonists along with livestock, seeds, and provisions to establish a colony in the New World. Their son, Snorri Thorfinnsson, was born a year later in a place called Vinland, probably in modern Newfoundland. The Vinland Sagas written two centuries later describe the family as the first Europeans to attempt permanent settlement in the Americas. After three years in their new home they found they could not combat Native American hostility and returned to Iceland. Here they settled on a farm in Glaumbær. Thorfinn sailed to Norway and sold Vinland goods at a handsome profit.

Migration to North America

Between 1815 and 1914 about 15,000 Icelanders, out of a total population of 75,000 people, emigrated to North America. Those that migrated to the United States settled primarily in Utah at first due to the Mormon connection. In 1875 the governor-general of Canada provided Icelanders with a large piece of land northwest of Winnipeg called the New Iceland Colony. It proved to be a difficult place to settle and most of the Icelanders went to Winnipeg and the northern Midwest in Wisconsin, Minnesota, and the Dakota Territories where land was readily available. Icelanders are also found in Saskatchewan and Nova Scotia. Michigan was merely a transit point and never a major destination.

As with most immigrants, Icelanders left their homeland for a variety of reasons. Religion caused the first Icelanders to emigrate to the United States in the 1850s. They were converts to the Church of Jesus Christ of Latter-day Saints or Mormonism and migrated to Utah. These immigrants were skilled artisans, builders, and farmers. A fair-sized Icelandic population remains in Utah to the present day.

A series of unfortunate events in the coming years acted to drive many Icelanders from their homes. In 1875 an eruption of the volcano Askja spread a layer of ash over the land, which interfered with farming and grazing. This was followed by a spell of cold weather. In 1881 and 1882 the temperature was below 35°F on average throughout the year and continued this way for several years. In the midst of this the island was hit with a measles epidemic.

In addition to these natural disasters, the people had little opportunity to improve their lives. There was a total lack of light industry and little opportunity for economic improvement. Finally, although there was a nationalistic revival on the island, the struggle continued toward political independence.

Chain migration was an important factor in Icelandic migration. In 1856 a Danish immigrant, William Wickmann, who had worked in southern Iceland, visited Milwaukee, Wisconsin. He wrote to friends in Iceland describing life in Wisconsin and in particular he mentioned the abundance of coffee. Especially fond of coffee, this triggered an out-migration. Later four Icelanders moved north from Milwaukee and settled on Washington Island in Lake Michigan, just north of the Door Peninsula above Green Bay. Others followed and settled in Minnesota. At one point in 1874 a group of Icelandic immigrants contacted the federal government seeking an island off the coast of Alaska as a new homeland. This idea did not settle well with officials in Washington, DC. Others plied their fishing and boat building trades in Washington's Puget Sound.

In the 1870s the Canadian government sought immigrants to fill a largely empty country and actively worked to secure Icelandic immigrants. They were given a large piece of land to the northwest of Winnipeg, Manitoba, which they named New Iceland. Here they could live in splendid isolation and maintain their traditional culture. Unfortunately, poor weather conditions, outbreaks of smallpox, and religious disputes caused many to leave and move to Winnipeg and even into the Dakotas. With the assistance of German and Norwegian immigrants they eventually created the largest Icelandic settlement in America in North Dakota.

Icelanders in Michigan

As mentioned previously, Michigan was a transit point for most Icelandic immigrants. In 1883 it was noted in a federal report that the immigration offices at Port Huron and Detroit recorded the arrival of Icelanders. Between 1880 and 1920 names like Guermander and Dagbartt Johnason, Elph Freeman, Adam and Anne Graboske, Albert and Augusta Ambjornson, Bary Brynjolfrion, and Oscar Hoffman rather accidentally appear on the enumerated census sheets with "Iceland" written after their names. This is rare because since Iceland at the time was part of Denmark, Icelanders were usually identified as Danish.

In 1872 Icelander Arni Gudmundsen wrote a letter to his mother in which he shared his immigrant experiences. Gudmundsen arrived in Québec City and took the railroad across Canada to Port Huron, Michigan, which was a point of entry into the United States. He planned on going to Washington Island where earlier Icelanders had settled and "farmed a little, [and] fished a lot," but he was concerned as he heard little work was available. Despite this concern, he continued toward the Midwest along with several other immigrant Icelanders. Due to a lack of funds, they traveled in the last and most likely the worst car of the train. Sleeping accommodations were either on hard benches or on the floor. Frequent train stops added to the uncomfortable travel experience. Needing money, they learned that track layers were readily hired along the line. So they stopped to make some money. The grinding work and a harsh foreman convinced the impoverished men after just half a day of work that better employment conditions probably existed ahead of them.

When they arrived in Muskegon, Michigan, they found jobs at a lumber mill. Earning two dollars a day, the men hoped to make enough money to avoid being a burden to the folks on Washington Island. The immigrants persevered for a short time, but the heat and humidity of the summer discouraged them and they headed west. The new environmental conditions befuddled many of the Icelanders. The Midwestern summer heat and humidity, as well as a myriad of insects besides the familiar mosquito, were things that they had to adjust to in their new homes.

Other Icelanders crossing Michigan had more deadly results. On August 29, 1873, a group of Icelandic immigrants was riding in the rear and cheapest car of a train crossing the state. In the vicinity of Muir in west Michigan, in Ionia County, because of an error by the flagman, the train, which was disabled due to mechanical failure, was rear-ended by a freight train. Two mothers and their two children were killed in the wreck and eleven other Icelanders were injured in the accident. The train wreck was one of Michigan's first serious train disasters.

These negative experiences did not deter some Icelanders from remaining in Michigan. They followed the typical Icelandic pattern of immigration and settlement. Most came in the late nineteenth century, many of them through Canada with their families, and settled in areas of close proximity to each other in Michigan. While the women remained in the home keeping house and raising the children, the men found work in rail car shops, sawmills, and furnaces. One worked as a millwright in a machine shop and others were employed as carpenters, bricklayers, and servants.

Due to an error made by a 1910 census taker, we have some specific information about a family of Icelandic immigrants in Chippewa County's Superior Township. The census taker first recorded the Jensen family as being from "Iceland" and then replaced it with "Denmark." Twenty-eight-year-old Sarah Jensen had immigrated with her husband, John, and their three-year-old son, John Jr., to the United States in 1878. This Icelandic family continued to speak and preserve their ancient language in their new American home. In the spring of 1910 John Jr., now thirty-five years old, was a grocery salesman living with his Canadian-born wife Jennett and their three children, all

Michigan-born since 1903. His brother Sigge, who had been born in Canada in 1888, was working as a log raftsman on the Waiska River guiding logs to the sawmill at Brimley. Fortunately this census "error" that accidentally listed Icelanders provides us with a small insight into the lives of a number of Icelandic immigrants in the Eastern Upper Peninsula. Naturally there were many more Icelanders but their stories get "lost" among the Danes.

Icelanders in 1930

For the first time in 1930 the federal census used "Iceland" rather than "Denmark" as the origin of these immigrants and thus we are able to get a better insight into these immigrants in Michigan who at that time numbered around thirty individuals. Although the first Icelanders arrived in 1882, per the census, the larger number arrived between 1910 and 1924, attracted to Michigan by the prosperity credited to the expanding automobile industry. Some of the immigrants first landed in Canada, settled there, married and then pushed westward into Michigan.

In the spring of 1930 seventeen Icelandic male immigrants were living in the Detroit Metropolitan area and working in the auto industry doing assembly and inspection. A number of Icelandic women were married to non-Icelanders who were employed in the auto industry as well. The majority of immigrants in Detroit were skilled workers in areas such as construction, carpentry, drayage, sailing, and commercial fishing. A tiny professional group included Finmur Finnson, the editor of a magazine, and Samuel Sigurdson, a real estate proprietor. Otherwise the immigrants were scattered across the state. Although nine of the eleven female immigrants in Michigan were married, two of them were self-employed: Susie Kanda operated a beauty salon and Gertrude Finson practiced osteopathic medicine in Battle Creek. The majority of Icelandic immigrants had skilled positions but a few did not—there was a night watchman at the Flint street car company, those who worked odd jobs, and one immigrant was unemployed. In terms of housing many of the men were boarders and in two cases were lodged by a Danish and Finnish family.

Life for Icelandic immigrants had its problems as they adjusted and assimilated into American life. Michigan's relatively hot and humid climate in the summer was disliked by many who grew up in the cool and cloudy summers of Iceland. The winter provided some respite where on December 21—the shortest day of the year—there are eight or nine hours of sunlight in Michigan, while in Iceland the hours of sunlight are half of that. It was also difficult for immigrants to learn English. Recent immigrants like Halldor Egilsson of Menominee, Michigan, who was a teenager in the 1960s, were greatly aided in learning English by programming on Marquette television station WLUC.

One benefit of life in America was the variety and abundance of food. In Iceland, fish dominated the diet with lamb a second but distant choice. Fermented shark, salted cod, and lamb head were now culinary items of the past.

Although these Icelandic immigrants were few in number they easily interacted with their Scandinavian neighbors who were their larger support group. However, it should be noted that since the Icelandic population was small, usually individuals had to struggle to maintain their traditions. The Lutheran and Unitarian churches, which most Icelanders belonged to, were found in most Michigan communities, as were Scandinavian mutual beneficial societies. Between 1882 and 1963 St. Peter's Danish Lutheran Evangelical Church in Detroit served the Scandinavian community. Until 1921 services were held in Danish. The Danish Brotherhood, organized in 1882, provided both Danes and Icelanders with a cultural and social outlet, especially for recent arrivals. There were lodges in Muskegon, Ludington, Menominee, Greenville, Frankfort, Edmore, Sidney, and Grand Rapids. The same was true of the Danish Sisterhood that was founded in Negaunee in 1883. Other Scandinavian organizations were available to the tiny Icelandic community—the Danish Old People's Home in Rochester; the American-Scandinavian Foundation, founded in 1910, which linked people culturally and socially; the Norse Civic Association, founded in Detroit in 1934, which provided closer unity and cooperation and focused on educational scholarships; and finally the Scandinavian Symphony Society of Detroit, established in 1930.

As is true for many small immigrant groups, it was common for Icelanders to maintain their heritage and linguistic and cultural traditions. The "West Icelanders," as Icelandic immigrants are known in the Old Country, can trace their genealogies back to the 900s in perfect Icelandic language. However, living in the United States has caused them to mix Icelandic with English words unknown in Icelandic. Two Icelandic newspapers, *Lögberg* (1888) and

Heimskringla (1886), were published in Winnipeg and could be subscribed to by Michigan Icelanders. This would provide them with updates and links to affairs in their former homes and to activities in North America. In 1959 these newspapers were combined, along with their names, and the combined paper is still published (although now mostly in English and focusing on news events and culture). In 1918 the Icelandic League of North America was established in Winnipeg and has always been at the forefront of most public spirited and cultural events among the Icelandic people in Canada and the United States.

For many years the Icelandic community in North America felt that there was a need to establish an Icelandic heritage museum where the ethnic experience, heritage, and culture could be fostered and preserved. The process began in the mid-1970s and was some twenty years in the making. The result is the New Iceland Heritage Museum in Gimli, Manitoba.

Educational Experience

Throughout the years a variety of Michigan colleges and universities have been attracted to Iceland and have in turn attracted Icelandic students to their campuses. In the nineteenth century, the University of Michigan led a number of scientific expeditions to Iceland. Today the University of Michigan Press publishes monographs on Iceland. William I. Miller, a professor of law at the university, has specialized in the study of the development of medieval Icelandic law. Michigan and other universities in the state have developed study abroad programs to Iceland and they study Iceland's unique geology. Icelandic students have attended many of the universities in the state and have returned to their homeland as prominent engineers. Some Icelandic Americans became professors, like Beatrice Gislasson Boynton who taught mathematics at Northern Michigan University and was influential in sponsoring a number of Icelandic immigrants to Michigan in the 1960s.

Icelandic Christmas

Christmas is the major Icelandic holiday. It is usually celebrated on December 12 and then for the twelve days between Christmas and January 6, the day of the coming of the Three Kings. Shoes are placed in the window and for good children they are filled with treats by one of thirteen Icelandic Santa Clauses, called jólasveinar or Yuletide Lads. Bad children are left a potato. The Yuletide Lads begin to arrive on December 12 and gradually leave by January 6. Adults feast on hangikjöt (smoked lamb) and Icelandic pancakes or crepes. This continues to be a time when a bottle of treasured brennivin (type of caraway-flavored schnapps made with potato pulp) is brought out and enjoyed by all. Some of these traditions were maintained in Michigan, especially the making of pancakes and sampling of brennivin.

Icelanders who settled in small numbers in Michigan are typical of the large and small immigrant groups that settled in the state. The 1940 U.S. Census showed that there were forty-three Icelandic immigrants in Michigan. Even this miniscule number of immigrants and their Michigan-born children provided their skills and labor to further the development of the state. They also brought with them important traditions and attitudes from the Old Country that go into making Michigan the diverse state it has become with rich ethnic cultures. The development of multiculturalism in Michigan and elsewhere has caused many third- and fourth-generation Icelandic Americans to revive an interest in their traditions and heritage, although learning to speak Icelandic is a difficult task for those who try.

Archives and Libraries

Danes

Bentley Historical Library, University of Michigan, Ann Arbor, Michigan. Contains a variety of materials on Danish immigrants and the depository of St. Peter Danish Evangelical Lutheran Church (1880–1980) in both Danish and English. For more information, see http:/www.bentley.umich.edu.

Central Upper Peninsula and University Archives, Northern Michigan University, Marquette, Michigan. See the Howard L. Nicholson Papers and extensive newspaper collection on microfilm for the Upper Peninsula. For more information, see http://www.nmu.edu/archives/.

Danish American Archive and Library (DAAL), Blair, Nebraska. Once located on the campus of now-defunct Dana College, the archives and library have moved to new quarters and have a community partnership with the University of Nebraska at Omaha. This is an extremely important collection of materials dealing with Danish immigration and consists of papers, photographs, and films. It is the repository of the Danish Brotherhood of America, the Danish Sisterhood of America, and the American Society of Danish Engineers. It has the most complete collection of the newspaper *Den Danske Pioneer.* This is considered the best Danish immigrant collection of archival materials. For more information, see http://www. danishamericanarchive.com.

Danish American Heritage Society, Salem, Oregon. The society's goal is the preservation of the history and culture of the Danish American experience. Twice a year they publish *The Bridge*, a historical journal. They work closely with the Danish American Archives and Library, the Danish Immigrant Museum, and the Danish Immigration Archives. For more information, see http://www.danishamericanheritagesociety.org.

Danish Immigrant Museum and International Cultural Center, Elk Horn, Iowa. The museum opened in 1994 and has over 35,000 artifacts and ongoing exhibits. For more information, see http://www.danishmuseum.org.

Danish Immigration Archives, Aalborg, Denmark. Established in 1932, this is a major resource that should be consulted. For more information, see http://emiarch.dk/home.

Danish Immigrant Archives-Grand View, Grand View University, Des Moines, Iowa. The Grand View Danish Immigrant Archives houses a wide variety of information sources related to the Danish immigrant influence on the United States, including personal histories, photographs, writings, and a large collection of Danish-American newspapers and magazines. The majority of the collection is focused around three main areas: the founding of Grand View and its early history, the Danish American immigrant experience, and N. F. S. Grundtvig.

Detroit Public Library, Burton Historical Collection, Detroit, Michigan. Contains newspaper clippings and obituaries, city directories, county histories, Detroit newspapers on microfilm, and photographs. For more information, see http://www.detroit.lib.mi.us/featuredcollection/burton-historical-collection.

Family History and Genealogy Center, Elk Horn, Iowa. The center opened in 1996 and has a fine collection of genealogical materials in the library. They provide translation services. It is part of the Danish Immigration Museum.

Flat River Historical Museum, Greenville, Michigan. The museum was established in 1967 and one of its major goals is to preserve the history of Danish immigration in Michigan. It is a useful resource on local Danish settlement. For more information, see http://flatriverhistoricalsociety.org.

Fremont Area District Library, Fremont, Michigan. Another repository of materials dealing with local Danish immigration.

Grant Public Library, Grant, Michigan. Its files contain information on local

Danish immigration. For more information, see http://www.grantlibrary. net.

Manistee County Historical Museum, Manistee, Michigan. Immigration materials for the area are to be found under "Danish Files."

Marquette Regional History Center, Marquette, Michigan. The John M. Longyear Library is a leading research center in the Upper Peninsula. It has a "Danish File," census data, photographs, and local newspapers on microfilm. For more information, see http://www.marquettehistory.org.

Mason County Historical Society/Historic White Pine Village, Ludington, Michigan. The story of Danish immigration can be found at this village site under "Danish Files." For more information, see www.historicwhitepinevillage.org.

White Cloud Community Library, White Cloud, Michigan. The vertical file holds papers from the Ashland Danish Folk School. For more information, see http://www.whitecloudlibrary.net.

Icelanders

Central Upper Peninsula and University Archives, Northern Michigan University, Marquette, Michigan. Contains oral interviews and paper materials. For more information, see http://www.nmu.edu/archives/.

Consulate of Iceland, Grosse Pointe Farms, Michigan.

Detroit Public Library, Burton Historical Collection, Detroit, Michigan. Contains newspaper clippings and obituaries. For more information, see http://www.detroit.lib.mi.us/featuredcollection/burton-historical-collection.

Fiske Petrarch Collection, Cornell University Library's Division of Rare and Manuscript Collections, Ithaca, New York. Holds a rare and extensive collection of books related to Iceland. For more information, see http://rmc. library.cornell.edu/collector/petrarch/index.html. Icelandic Emigration Center, Hofsós, Iceland. Has genealogy service and library facilities. For more information, see en.hofsos.is.

New Iceland Heritage Museum, Gimli, Manitoba. Contains a research library and museum artifacts.

Recipes

Danish Recipes

The following recipes were provided by Allan Johnsen, a recent Danish immigrant to Michigan's Upper Peninsula.

Danish Pancakes

1¼ cups of flour	¼ tsp. of salt
1¼ cups of milk	⅓ cup of melted butter
2 eggs	1 Tbsp. of oil for frying

Whisk everything together in a bowl until creamy. Pour pancake batter in a hot frying pan. Serve with jam, powdered sugar, or regular sugar.

Dark Rye Bread (Rugbrød)

1 cup of leavened flour	1½ cups of linseed
7 cups of broken rye seeds	1½ cups of sunflower seeds
4¼ cups of water	1 malt beer (preferably Danish beer)
4 cups of wheat flour	2 Tbsp. of sugar
2 Tbsp. of salt	4 cups of coarse rye flour

Day One: Mix leavened flour, rye seeds, water, wheat flour, salt, linseed, and sunflower seeds. You should have a liquid batter. Let stand at room temperature for twenty-four hours.

Day Two: Take one cup of the mass and set it aside. Mix malt, sugar, and rye flour together into the remaining dough. Make the consistency thick. Pour it into two deep and lubricated bread pans and let them raise at room temperature for six hours. Cover with a wet dish towel. Before putting in the oven, prick the top in several places with a fork. Bake for two hours at 400°F. Let cool for two hours.

Buttermilk Soup (Koldskål)

2 eggs

2 Tbsp. of sugar

2 Tbsp. of lemon juice

3 cups of buttermilk

Whisk the eggs for two minutes. Add sugar and continue whisking. Add lemon juice and buttermilk. Mix. Refrigerate and enjoy as a refreshing drink. Serve with Nilla Wafers in it and eat it like a soup if you wish.

"Poor Man's Entree" (Skrædderduelse)

1½ lbs. of smoked bacon cut into small pieces

4 medium-sized onions cut into slices

1½–2 cups of cream

Pinch of pepper

Pinch of salt

Chives and parsley as decoration

Cook the bacon in a pan until it is crunchy. Remove most of the fat. Take the bacon out of the pan and sauté the onions until they are golden brown. Add the bacon back into the pan and pour cream in. Occasionally stir as the sauce simmers on medium heat. Taste test and add salt and pepper if needed. Decorate with chives or parsley and serve with potatoes.

Millionbof

1 lb. of ground beef	1 tsp. of paprika
2 onions	2 Tbsp. of flour
Approximately 4 Tbsp. of butter	Water
Approximately 1½ cups of beef stock	Brown food coloring
Pinch of salt and freshly ground pepper	

Peel and chop onions. Melt the butter in a pan and sauté the onions. Add the ground beef and keep stirring it until it's cooked. Add the beef stock, salt, pepper, and paprika. Let it simmer at low heat while covered for about thirty minutes. Make a thickener out of water and flour and add it to the pan. Bring the contents of the pan to a boil for five minutes. Add a few drops of brown food coloring. Serve it with mashed potatoes or egg noodles.

Danish Meatballs (Frikadeller)

2 slices of white bread without crust	2 tsp. of salt
1 cup of water or milk	½ tsp. of pepper
1 onion	1½ lbs. of lean ground beef
1 egg	Butter or margarine

Put the slices of bread into a soup bowl and soak them in water or milk for about five minutes. Mix onions, eggs, salt, and pepper with the bread mixture and then add the meat. Put some of the butter in a pan. As soon as they are brown on one side turn them and do the same thing to the other side. Place the brown meatballs in a pan that will go into a preheated oven set to 300°F and bake them for twenty minutes. They can be served with many dishes.

Fried Twists (Klejner)

3 eggs	Grated lemon rind
½ lb. of melted butter	1½ lbs. of wheat flour
½ lb. of sugar	¼ cup of cognac or brandy
3 Tbsp. of cream	Oil for boiling

Mix the eggs and sugar until you no longer hear any crunching noises. Add the cooled, melted butter and mix. Add cream, lemon rind, and cognac and mix. Add half of the flour bit by bit. Keep adding flour until the dough becomes firm. Let the dough cool for thirty minutes. Roll the dough out with a rolling pin on a flour-covered surface. Roll out as thin as possible. Proceed to cut the cookies using a pastry cutter and twist the klejner into the right shape.

Heat the oil in a pot to 350°F. Place the klejner in the oil, three or four at a time, until they are golden brown. Lay them on parchment paper. When they are cold they can be eaten.

Icelandic Recipes

Permission to print these Icelandic recipes has been generously provided by Audrey Juve Kwasnica of the Winnipeg-based Icelandic Canadian newspaper, *Lögberg-Heimskringla*.

Baked Whitefish

4 cups bread crumbs, crushed	2 tsp. salt
½ cup butter, melted	¼ tsp. pepper
¼ cup finely minced onion	1 tsp. sage or thyme
Apple (if desired)	Poultry seasoning to taste

First clean fish, then stuff cavity with bread crumb dressing.

Mix bread crumbs and melted butter. Fry until light brown, stirring to prevent browning too much. Mix spices in lightly. For a moist stuffing add hot water. Cool and place stuffing in fish cavity, then sew up.

Place fish in shallow pan, sprinkle with salt and pepper and melted butter. Bake for 1 to 1¼ hours at 350°F.

Red Cabbage

1 small head red cabbage	3 cloves
3 Tbsp. raspberry jam	1¼ ounce butter
2 red apples	1 cup chicken broth

1–2 tsp. red wine vinegar   ½ cup red wine

1 Tbsp. sugar

Slice the red cabbage thinly. Place in a pot. Cut apples into chunks. Add all other ingredients except the red wine. Cook for 45 minutes. Add red wine. Take off heat.

Fruit Soup (Sæt Súpa)

13 cups water

1 cup fruit juice (raspberry, strawberry, or cowberry)

¾ cup sago or slow-cooking tapioca

1–2 sticks cinnamon or ½–1 tsp. ground cinnamon

½ cup raisins

1 tsp. salt

1 cup prunes

10–15 drops lemon juice

¾ cup sugar

Soak sago overnight. Drop cinnamon stick in cold water and bring to a boil. Add sago (after soaking), stirring constantly. Boil ½ hour. Add raisins and prunes. Cook until soup is clear (½ hour). Remove cinnamon sticks. Add fruit juice before serving. Serve hot or cold, as a dessert.

Pancakes (Pönnukökur)

2 eggs	½ cup sour cream or buttermilk
⅓ cup sugar	1½ cups sifted all-purpose flour
¼ tsp. salt	1 tsp. baking powder
½ tsp. vanilla	½ tsp. baking soda
½ tsp. cinnamon	2 cups sweet milk

Beat eggs. Add sugar, salt, vanilla, and cinnamon. Combine and sift flour, baking powder, and baking soda.

Add sour cream or buttermilk and sifted dry ingredients to egg mixture and mix until smooth. Gradually stir in sweet milk.

To bake, use a hot, lightly greased griddle. Preheat griddle, then lift off heat while you pour about ⅕ cup of batter on it. Fry both sides. Regrease pan lightly with butter each time. Makes about 2 dozen. Spread with white or brown sugar and roll.

Christmas Loaf (Jólakaka)

2 eggs	1 cup sugar
⅛ lb. butter	1 cup milk
3 cups flour	1 tsp. baking powder
1 cup raisins	Pinch salt
½ tsp. cardamom (pulverized)	¼ cup citron peel

Cream butter and sugar. Add eggs and milk, flour, and baking powder, raisins, peel, and cardamom.

Mix well and beat briskly for a few minutes. Bake in a slow oven for one hour at 325°F, using a loaf pan.

Caraway Coffee (Kúmenkaffi)

Brew some good, strong coffee. If you use ready-ground, add some caraway seeds before brewing. If you grind your own, throw some caraway seeds in the grinder along with the coffee beans. People's tastes vary widely where coffee is concerned, and the amount of caraway should be adjusted to taste.

For a truly adult version of caraway coffee, make a "Black Russian" with fresh, hot coffee and use *brennivin* (Icelandic alcoholic liquor) instead of vodka. To add a bit of brennivin is a tradition still honored by some Icelanders, and there are stories of caraway coffee sometimes arousing the happy suspicion that the hostess has put "a little something extra" in the coffee.

Burning Wine (Brennivin)

Brennivin is the national liquor of Iceland and is made with fermented potato pulp and flavored with caraway seed. Because of its high alcoholic content it is referred to as "black death." It is similar to Scandinavian *akvavit*, while the Danes have a similar drink called *brændevin*.

Immigrant Letters

etters from Knud Nielsen of Menominee, Michigan, to his girlfriend and future wife, Maren Nielsen. John W. and Elizabeth Nielsen collection, Danish American Archives and Library (DAAL), Blair, Nebraska.

Menominee, Michigan, May 8, 1893

I am in Menominee now and have begun to work again, and I am in good shape. I work only 10 hours and after that my time is my own, and I am not working so hard. I am doing the same as last summer, namely sorting the boards as they come out of the mill.

The World Exposition in Chicago has opened. Oh it would be wonderful to go and see what the different countries have brought in. They say it's very beautiful, but I won't go there. It is too expensive.

Menominee, December 1, 1895

Dear Friend,

I am very glad each time you write to me because now I want to tell you what I have long felt, but at the time I went abroad I thought you were too young to make a decision, but now I hope you can make your own decision. **73**

I have loved you for many years and hoped that you were not uninterested in me. And now I want to ask you if you would be willing to share your future with me through our lives. I have, for a long time, put things on paper, but as it will likely be some years before I can get back to Denmark I dared not wait any longer. If this is too long a time for you to wait and to ask as you have not seen me in 3 and half years and know how I have behaved, but I love you enough to behave myself properly from day to day to make you happy in so far as my ability and earning ability will permit. My friend if you cannot answer my feelings then let me remain your friend whatever the feelings but I would be happy if your response is yes.

Menominee, December 8, 1895

I am well but there is hard times this winter. Work has almost stopped all around us and there is great need among the miners in many places. I hardly think I will work in the forest this winter because the payment is so little that I can hardly pay. The pay is sixteen dollars a month, and we have to work like an ox—much harder than when they pay $26.00 for the same work.

No Date

I see you have received what I sent, but the photo was really for you, but since you sent it home, let them keep it and I expect to send you another this summer. The ribbon on the jacket is a sign of membership in a society. You asked how I managed to send it. There was a fellow here from around Horsens who went home [to Denmark] for a visit intending then to go on to South Africa. He took it along. I expect my brother to visit me this month. There is a church meeting in this state that he has to attend.

You ask me what I am working with. It is a machine that produces electric sparks, and that's the best explanation I can give. It gets too involved. Yes the U.S. is at war with Spain near the Philippines. . . . . . They [the Spaniards] are devils more than human beings in what they have done to Cuba. For my sake don't be afraid. They have more than enough soldiers without me. Some have even been sent home for that reason.

Yes I remember our farewell in the west room and many other things from the time gone by. You are my beloved girl and my bride-to-be.

No Date

I have received your letter and photograph. I wish you were here so they could see I am not the woman-hater they think I am, but I suppose they will keep that belief for awhile yet.

I can tell you I got first prize for my steam engine and my generator at an exhibition in town, and now I am working on an electric motor, that is, a machine that can change electricity into power, but it could be a question whether it will work or not, because I am only a student, but it's hard to get a teacher. If I have luck with it I'll take it along home so you get to see it. You don't need to fear, I am not exaggerating my studies, because it is just a hobby, what we used to call handicraft. It takes some money...

Better than to go to the bar as most of the men do. That takes even more money and is the ruin of oneself. I am ok otherwise. I work 12 hours a day at the saw mill now and have been for awhile.

Menominee, August 25, 1895

... Today I have been learning to ride a bicycle. It's not mine, just an old one that I did some fixing on. I think my cousin and I will buy one jointly next spring when they get cheaper. It would be fun to ride out in the country next summer, once in awhile. You say it will probably be machine work I will do when I get home, but I don't know if that is possible, but at least in my spare time I would do it. If I do get any spare time, it probably won't be as much as here. I have to admit I don't know anything about what I will do at home, but I suppose there will be something. You write that you haven't heard from my brother since April, I haven't heard for a long time either. This time it isn't my fault because I wrote last.

Menominee, October 20, 1896

Everything here is at a standstill because of the presidential election. The two parties are fighting for dominance, and poor people suffer under all of it. But I hope it will get better when their fighting is over. . . . . . my little friend . . .

Menominee, July 22, 1897

My Beloved Girl,

You write that Inner Mission and the Grundtvigians have had a falling out; and that doesn't surprise me. Tell me which one you favor. I believe that your parents have not had much to do with Inner Mission people. I don't believe their views are very healthy. There's too much that's judgmental and damnation [in their preaching]. And these itinerant preachers should not be. They are mostly people who [don't] work hard or work at all. The Grundtvigian view I like better. They want people to have a good and healthy enlightenment instead of being hustled into heaven with ghosts. This is probably enough of that, and maybe you don't agree with me. If that is so, I ask you tell me and I won't bring up that subject again.

I send you a sample of the star spangled banner, which I love next best to our dear Dannebrog. They are both flags of freedom. . . . and they look nice side by side.

Menominee, September 12, 1898

They say here that I am a woman hater. I think they are wrong, but I let them think what they will. I see your brother is free from the military uniform and that is good. I am no friend of militarism, and in many cases the times spent as a soldier is wasted. Besides in case of war Denmark is unfortunately the little one.

I believe I'll have steady work this winter at the work place if all goes well. Winter is at the door . . . here in town they do pass more quickly than in the woods. When I'm up there I constantly long for the town. Maybe I won't get there anymore. I hope all of you will welcome me when I come to Denmark, especially you.

Menominee, October 2, 1899

I have so much to do in my spare time. Right now I am making a telegraph instrument, so I can teach myself to send telegrams if I don't get tired. ...I have to make a telephone instrument too if I get time. Regarding postponing of my trip home I don't plan to do that unless something happens that I don't know today. People here will be rather surprised because no one knows it till

I am almost ready to go. Most of them say I am a woman hater, but I don't think you believe that, my dear girl.

Menominee, December 30, 1900

I am glad you're enjoying your stay at the [folk] high school as I thought you would. There's hardly anyone that isn't pulled along. I wish I had been there or could get there, but when I had time, I had no money, and now it's the opposite. A stay there would have been good for me. It was great that you could be home for Christmas. Thank you for the tie clasp and buttons [cufflinks] you sent and thanks to your mother for the stockings. They fit fine.

I haven't decided what month I leave. I have to be concerned about the man I work for, but there's still time before spring.

Menominee, May 28, 1900

My Beloved Maren,

I see you have gone over to Inner Mission. My dear girl, why you too? I could hardly believe my eyes. I remember your parents were against it when I was home. Is there nothing better than this narrow-minded and judgmental sect to be found in Denmark? And all their so-called inner missionaries that make speeches they don't even understand themselves. Excuse me, but those who are in it can't and won't see it, but most of them live at the expense of others to avoid working. Is there a lack of pastors in Denmark? Why don't you good people look at the [folk] high schools with their freedom of spirit and healthy outlook on life? They can't threaten a sinner into God's heaven. I am far from angry with you. You have your own freedom in this as in everything else. I want freedom and grant it also to you. If you are happy there, I suppose it is best I doubt I can follow you, but I'll try to be just so it has as little effect on our life together as possible, and also on our happiness. It's probably better not to write any more about this. . . . Your fiancée,

Knud Nielsen

You mustn't take this as a scolding sermon because it isn't meant that way.

Menominee, March 12, 1901

. . . Will you send me the measure of your foot? I have thought you should have a pair of American shoes so you can see what our shoemakers can do.

I still haven't decided when I will leave and I probably won't until just before I leave.

Menominee, September 12, 1901

Sometimes I can hardly believe that it can be so long since I came to this town one morning late in April. I stood at the depot without being able to speak to people with an address that was useless. Those I showed it to didn't know the man and the streets had no name [signs] and the houses no numbers. Everything has really changed. We have electric streetcars and everything else that belongs to an up-and-coming town. It's like that almost everywhere here and no European can imagine how quickly everything moves.

I am thinking to come for Christmas but I can't say for sure. I can't leave till early December very well, but if everything goes well, that would work.

Notes

1. Information in the introduction is drawn from Knud J. V. Jespersen, *A History of Denmark*, trans. Ivan Hill (New York: Palgrave Macmillan, 2004); Steward Oakley, *A Short History of Denmark* (New York: Praeger Publishers, 1972); Kristian Hvidt, *Flight to America: The Social Background of 300,000 Danish Emigrants* (New York: Academic Press, 1975); Howard B. Furer, *The Scandinavians in America, 986–1970: A Chronology and Fact Book* (Dobbs Ferry, NY: Oceana Publications, 1972).

2. Kendric Babcock, *The Scandinavian Element in the United States* (New York: Arno Press, 1969).

3. Jespersen, *A History Denmark*, 140.

4. Frederick Hale, *Danes in North America* (Seattle: University of Washington Press, 1984), xiv.

5. Hvidt, *Flight to America*, 174.

6. Ibid., 175.

7. Information in "Danish Religion, Folks Schools, and Fraternal Organizations" is drawn from Rosena Morin and Dorothy Gerue, Danish settlement history, Howard L. Nicholson Papers. Central Upper Peninsula and University Archives, Northern Michigan University, unpublished, 2004 ; John H. Bille, *A History of the Danes in America* (San Francisco, CA: R and E Research Associates, 1971); Alfred O. Fonkalsrud, *The Scandinavian-American* (Minneapolis: K. C. Holter

Publishing, 1915); Jespersen, *A History of Denmark*; Birgit Flemming Larsen and Henning Bender, eds., *Danish Emigration to the U.S.A*, trans. Karen Veien (Aalborg, Denmark: Danes Worldwide Archives, 1992); Viggo Christofferson and Francis Christofferson, *Bethany Lutheran Church, 1878-1978* (Ludington, MI: Historic White Pine Village, 1978); Holger Rosenstand, *From the Land of the Great Lakes: Pioneer Days in Michigan*, trans. William R. Garred (Des Moines, IA: Danish Interest Conference, the Lutheran Church of America, 1981); Nancy Barlett, "Abandonment of Danish: A Case Study from Montcalm County Michigan" (senior thesis, University of Michigan, 1979).

8. Bille, *A History of the Danes in America*, 3.

9. Fonkalsrud, *The Scandinavian-American*, 46-47.

10. Barlett, "Abandonment of Danish," 6.

11. Bille, *A History of the Danes in America*, 15.

12. Fonkalsrud, *The Scandinavian-American*, 46-47.

13. Rosenstand, *From the Land of the Great Lakes*, 224-229.

14. Barlett, "Abandonment of Danish," 6.

15. Information in "Danish Christmas" is drawn from the John W. and Elizabeth Nielsen collection, Danish American Archive and Library, Blair, NE; Tanya Gulevich, *Encyclopedia of Christmas* (Detroit, MI: Omnigraphics, 2000), 161-163.

16. John W. and Elizabeth Nielsen collection, Danish American Archives and Library, Blair, NE.

17. Information in "The Danish Folk School" is drawn from Chester A. Graham to Mr. Elliot, Historical Researcher, April 18, 1978, Grant Area District Library; Harold W. Stubblefield, "The Danish Folk High School and Its Reception in the United States, 1870s-1930s," http://www-distance.syr.edu/stubblefield.html; Grant Area District Library, *Grant Area Yesterday Today* (Dallas: Taylor Publishing, 1979); Alice Stengren, "A Danish Settlement in Grant, Michigan," unpublished paper, Central Michigan University, 1970, White Cloud Community Library; Enok Mortensen, *Schools for Life: A Danish-American Experiment in Adult Education* (Askov, MN: Danish-American Heritage Society, 1977); Enok Mortensen, *Stories from Our Church: A Popular History of the Danish Evangelical Lutheran Church of America* (Des Moines, IA: Committee on Publications of the Danish Evangelical Lutheran Church of America, 1952); Hvidt, *Flight to America*.

18. Barlett, "Abandonment of Danish," 9-10.

19. Grant Area District Library, *Grant Area Yesterday Today*, 75.

20. Ibid.

21. Ibid., 35.

22. Ibid., 46.

23. Mortensen, *Schools for Life*, 48–49.

24. Chester A. Graham to Mr. Elliot, Historical Researcher, April 18, 1978, Grant Area District Library.

25. Grant Area District Library, *Grant Area Yesterday Today*, 38–63.

26. Information in "Danish Brotherhood" is drawn from Christian T. Feddersen, *Scandinavians in Michigan: With Special Reference to Detroit and Environs*, vol. 1 (Romeo, MI: self-published, 1968); The Danish Brotherhood in America, "Denmark Our Heritage, America Our Home," www.danishbrotherhood.ca; Mortensen, *Schools for Life*.

27. Furer, *Scandinavians in America*, 80.

28. Information in "Danish Sisterhood" is drawn from Marquette County Public Records, 1889; *R. L. Polk and Company's Manistee City Directory, 1910–1911* (Detroit, MI: R.L. Polk Publishers, 1910); The Danish Brotherhood in America, "Denmark Our Heritage, America Our Home," ; "Danish Sisterhood was Founded in Negaunee," *Mining Journal*, May 14, 1983; The Danish Sisterhood of America, "Excerpts from Our Founder Christine Hemmingsen's Husband's Diary," trans. Lizette Burtis, http://www.danishsisterhood.org/DanishHTML/history.asp; Feddersen, *Scandinavians in Michigan*.

29. Danish Sisterhood of America website.

30. Furer, *Scandinavians in America*, 63.

31. Information in "Montcalm County Danes" was found in the following: Feddersen, *Scandinavians in Michigan*; Jespersen, *A History of Denmark*; Larsen and Bender, *Danish Emigration to the U.S. A.*; August Rasmussen, *Pioneer Life in the Big Dane Settlement: Montcalm County, Michigan, 1856–1902* (Salt Lake City: Genealogical Society of Utah, 1976).

32. Rasmussen, *Pioneer Life*.

33. Ibid.

34. Ibid.

35. Barlett, "Abandonment of Danish," 28.

36. Information in "Detroit Danes" is drawn from Olaf Jensen and Evelyn Jensen, "Danish," in *Peoples of Michigan*, eds. James M. Anderson and Iva A. Smith, vol. 2, *Ethnic Groups in Michigan* (Detroit, MI: Ethnos Press, 1983), 94–95; Danish Immigrant Archives-Grand View, Des Moines, IA; Burton Historical Collection,

Detroit Public Library,, Detroit, MI; Charles E. Sorensen, *My Forty Years with Ford* (New York: Norton, 1956); Norman Beasley, *Knudsen: A Biography* (New York: Whittlesey House, 1947).

37. Wayne State University Department of Sociology and Anthropology, *Ethnic Groups in Detroit: 1951* (Detroit, MI: Wayne State University Department of Sociology and Anthropology, 1951).

38. Burton Historical Collection, Detroit Public Library, Detroit, MI.

39. Ibid.

40. Jensen and Jensen, "Danish," 94–95.

41. Burton Historical Collection, Detroit Public Library, Detroit, MI.

42. Jensen and Jensen, "Danish," 95.

43. Sorensen, *My Forty Years*, 40.

44. Ibid.

45. Information in "Muskegon Danes" is drawn from *History of Muskegon County Michigan, with Illustrations and Biographical Sketches of Some of Its Prominent Men and Pioneers* (Chicago: H. R. Page & Co., 1882).

46. Information in "Ludington Danes" is drawn from Mason County Historical Society/Historic White Pine Village, Ludington, Michigan.

47. Senator Robert and Marjorie Griffin, http://www.cmich.edu/academics/humanities_social_behavioral_sciences/CHSBSDepartments/CHSBS PoliticalScience /CHSBSPOLISCIGriffinEndowedChair/CHSBSPOLISCIGEC ---About/Pages/Senator-Robert-and-Marjorie-Griffin.aspx.

48. Information in "Manistee Danes" is drawn from Danish Files, Manistee County Historical Society, Manistee, MI; E. M. Favrholdt, *Labour in the Vineyard* (Cedar Falls, IA: Holst Printing Company, 1923); Nels Johnson, *The Century Tower Clocks for Churches, Court Houses, City Halls and Other Public Buildings. Fine Regulators and Electrical Dials for Banks, Railroads, Private Residences and Public Buildings. Manufactured by Nels Johnson, Manistee, Michigan, U.S.A.* (Manistee, MI: Manistee Printing Co., 1894); N. C. Madsen, *Danske i Amerika* (Minneapolis, MN: Rasmussen Publishing, 1916).

49. Favrholdt, *Labour in the Vineyard*.

50. Ibid.

51. Manistee County Historical Society.

52. Johnson, "History of the Life of Nels Johnson," Manistee County Historical Society.

53. Information in "Menominee Danes" is drawn from the John W. and Elizabeth

Nielsen collection, Danish American Archive and Library, Blair, NE.

54. John W. and Elizabeth Nielsen collection, Danish American Archive and Library, Blair, NE.

55. See appendix 3.

56. Hvidt, *Flight to America*, 83.

57. See appendix 3.

58. *Washington Post*, January 10, 1973.

59. All the information about Stephenson Danes is drawn from Rosena Morin and Dorothy Gerue, *The Danish Settlement.* Stephenson, MI: Family History, 2004.

60. Information in "Marquette County Danes" is drawn from United States Census Reports, U.S. Bureau of Census, 1850–1990, State of Michigan County Tables; Marquette County Court Record; *The Mining Journal*, 1912, 1913, 1932, 1966; Marquette Regional History Center.

For Further Reference

Danes

Andersen, Arlow W. *The Salt of the Earth: A History of Norwegian-Danish Methodism in America.* Nashville, TN: Parthenon Press, 1962.

Babcock, Kendric. *The Scandinavian Element in the United States.* New York: Arno Press, 1969.

Barlett, Nancy. "Abandonment of Danish: A Case Study from Montcalm County, Michigan." Senior thesis, University of Michigan, 1979.

Beasley, Norman. *Knudsen: A Biography.* New York: Whittlesey House, 1947.

Bille, John H. *A History of the Danes in America.* San Francisco, CA: R and E Research Associates, 1971.

Chrisman, Noel. *Ethnic Influences on Urban Groups: The Danish Americans.* PhD diss., University of California, 1966. San Francisco: R and E Research Associates, 1975.

Christensen, Russell and Carol Meyer. "The Christensen Family History." Howard L. Nicholson Papers. Central Upper Peninsula and University Archives, Northern Michigan University. Unpublished manuscript.

Christofferson, Viggo, and Francis Christofferson. *Bethany Lutheran Church, 1878–1978.* Ludington, MI: Historic White Pine Village, 1978.

Danish Brotherhood in America, "Denmark Our Heritage, America Our Home." www.danishbrotherhood.ca.

Danish Brotherhood Magazine. Blair, NE: Danish-American Archives and Library, 1882 to present.

Danish Sisterhood of America, "Excerpts from Our Founder Christine Hemmingsen's Husband's Diary." Translated by Lizette Burtis. http://www.danishsisterhood. org/DanishHTML/history.asp.

Danske i Amerika. Translated by volunteers at Dana College. Minneapolis, MN: Rasmussen Publishing, 1916.

Dasef, John W. *History of Montcalm County, Michigan: Its People, Industries and Institutions.* 2 vols. Indianapolis, IN: B. F. Brown, 1916.

Douglas, Lee V. *Danish Immigration to America: An Annotated Bibliography of Resources at the Library of Congress.* Research Guide No. 6. Washington, DC: Library of Congress, Local History and Genealogy Reading Room.

Eddy, Anna. "The Danish Sisterhood of America: DSS Founder's History Revealed." http://www.danishsisterhood.org/history.

———. "The Danish Sisterhood of America: The Early History of the Danish Sisterhood of America." http://www.danishsisterhood.org/earlyhistory.asp.

Favrholdt, E. M. *Labour in the Vineyard: Fifty-Five Years History of the Danish Lutheran Church in Manistee, Michigan 1868–1923.* Cedar Falls, IA: Holst Printing Co (for the Manistee Historical Society), 1923.

Feddersen, Christian T. *Scandinavians in Michigan: With Special Reference to Detroit and Environs,* vol. 1. Romeo, MI: self-published, 1968.

The Flat River Historical Society. *A History of the Greater Greenville Area: 1844 to 1994.* Dallas, TX: Taylor Publishing Company, 1994.

Fonkalsrud, Alfred O. *The Scandinavian-American.* Minneapolis: K. C. Holter Publishing, 1915.

Furer, Howard. *The Scandinavians in America, 986–1970: A Chronology and Fact Book.* Dobbs Ferry, NY: Oceana Publications, 1972.

Gerue, Dorothy. Deed family history. Howard L. Nicholson Papers. Central Upper Peninsula and University Archives, Northern Michigan University. Unpublished, 2004.

Grant Area District Library. *Grant Area Yesterday Today.* Dallas: Taylor Publishing, 1979.

Gulevich, Tanya. *Encyclopedia of Christmas.* Detroit, MI: Omnigraphics, 2000.

Hale, Frederick. *Danes in North America.* Seattle: University of Washington Press, 1984.

Hansen, Judith. *We Are a Little Land: Cultural Assumptions in Danish Everyday Life.*

New York: Arno Press, 1980.

Higgs, Robert. *The Transformation of the American Economy, 1865-1914.* New York: John Wiley, 1971.

History of Muskegon County Michigan with Illustrations and Biographical Sketches of Some of Its Prominent Men and Pioneers. Chicago: H. R. Page & Co., 1882.

Hoffenblad, Ludvig M. "Det danske Søstersamfund i Amerika." In *Dansk i Amerika.* Minneapolis, MN: C. Rasmussen Publishing, 1908.

Hvidt, Kristian. *Flight to America: The Social Background of 300,000 Danish Emigrants.* New York: Academic Press, 1975.

Jensen, Olaf, and Evelyn Jensen. "Danish." In *The Peoples of Michigan.* Vol. 2, *Ethnic Groups in Michigan,* eds. James M. Anderson and Iva A. Smith. Detroit, MI: Ethnos Press, 1983, pp. 94-95.

Jespersen, Knud J. V. *A History of Denmark.* Translated by Ivan Hill. New York: Palgrave Macmillan, 2004.

Johnsen, Allan. "Danish Recipes." Howard L. Nicholson Papers. Central Upper Peninsula and University Archives, Northern Michigan University.

Johnson, Nels. *The Century Tower Clocks for Churches, Court Houses, City Halls and other Public Buildings. Fine Regulators and Electric Dials for Banks, Railroads, Private Residences and Public Buildings. Manufactured by Nels Johnson, Manistee, Michigan, U.S.A.* Manistee, MI: Manistee Printing Company, 1894.

Kjølhede, Peder, P. S. Vig, and I. M. Hansen. *Danes in America: Danish-American Lutheranism from 1860 to 1908.* Edited by John W. Nielsen. Translated by Edward A. Hansen and Inga Larsen. Blair, NE: Lur Publications, 2001.

Larsen, Birgit Flemming, ed. *On Distant Shores: Proceedings of the Marcus Lee Hansen Immigration Conference.* Translated by Karen Veien. Aalborg, Denmark: Danes Worldwide Archives in collaboration with the Danish Society for Emigration History, 1993.

Larsen, Birgit Flemming, and Henning Bender, eds. *Danish Emigration to the U.S.A.* Translated by Karen Veien. Aalborg, Denmark: Danes Worldwide Archives, 1992.

Madsen, N. C. *Danske i Amerika.* Minneapolis, MN: C. Rasmussen Publishing, 1916.

McDonald, Julie. *Delectably Danish: Recipes and Reflections.* Iowa City, IA: Penfield Press, 1984.

Morin, Rosena, ed. *Letters to America.* Howard L. Nicholson Papers. Central Upper Peninsula and University Archives, Northern Michigan University. Unpublished, 1990.

Morin, Rosena and Dorothy Gerue. Danish settlement history. Howard L. Nicholson
    Papers. Central Upper Peninsula and University Archives, Northern Michigan
    University. Unpublished, 2004.

Mortensen, Enok. *The Danish Lutheran Church in America: The History and Heritage
    of the American Evangelical Lutheran Church*. Philadelphia, PA: Board of Publi-
    cation of the Lutheran Church in America, 1967.

——. *Schools for Life: A Danish-American Experiment in Adult Education*. Askov,
    MN: Danish-American Heritage Society, 1977.

——. *Stories from Our Church: A Popular History of the Danish Evangelical Lu-
    theran Church of America*. Des Moines, IA: Committee on Publications of the
    Danish Evangelical Lutheran Church of America, 1952.

Nelson, O. N., ed. *History of the Scandinavians and Successful Scandinavians in the
    United States*. New York: Haskell House Publishers, 1969.

Nordstrom, Byron J. *Scandinavia Since 1500*. Minneapolis: University of Minnesota
    Press, 2000.

Oakley, Steward. *A Short History of Denmark*. New York: Praeger Publishers, 1972.

Olson, Kay M. *Norwegian, Swedish, and Danish Immigrants: 1820–1920*. Mankato,
    MN: Blue Earth Books, 2002.

Pedersen, Lisbeth and Mads Andreasen. "The Escape to America." http://www.kal-
    mus.dk/html/august.html.

Rasmussen, August. *Pioneer Life in the Big Dane Settlement: Montcalm County,
    Michigan, 1856–1902*. Salt Lake City: Genealogical Society of Utah, 1976.

Ravnkilde, Knud. *From Fettered to Free: The Farmer in Denmark's History*. Hurst,
    Berkshire, England: Danish Language Services, 1989.

R. L. Polk and Company's Manistee City Directory, 1910–1911. Detroit, MI: R. L. Polk
    Publishers, 1910.

Robertson, Augustine M. *Indians, Sawmills and Danes: The Early History of the Flat
    River Area of Michigan*. Greenville, MI: Flat River Historical Society, 1971.

Rosenstand, Holger. *From the Land of the Great Lakes: Pioneer Days in Michigan*.
    Translated by William R. Garred. Des Moines, IA: Danish Interest Conference,
    Lutheran Church in America, 1981.

Sawyer, Alvah. *A History of the Northern Peninsula of Michigan and Its People, Its
    Mining, Lumber and Agricultural Industries*. 3 vols. Chicago, IL: The Lewis Pub-
    lishing Company, 1911.

Seller, Maxine, ed. *Immigrant Women*. Philadelphia, PA: Temple University Press,
    1981.

Skärdal, Dorothy Burton. "Danes." In *Harvard Encyclopedia of American Ethnic Groups*, ed. Stephen Thernstrom, Ann Orlov, and Oscar Handlin. London: The Belknap Press of Harvard University Press, 1981, pp. 273-282.

Sorensen, Charles E. *My Forty Years with Ford.* New York: Norton, 1956.

Stengren, Alice. "A Danish Settlement in Grant, Michigan." Unpublished paper. Central Michigan University, 1970. Newaygo County Historical Society.

Stilling, Niels and Anne Olsen. *A New Life.* Translated by Karen Veien. Aalborg, Denmark: Danes Worldwide Archives in collaboration with the Danish Society for Emigration History, 1994.

Stubblefield, Harold W. "The Danish Folk High School and Its Reception in the United States: 1870s-1930s." http://www-distance.syr.edu/stubblefield.html.

Thernstrom, Stephan, Ann Orlov, and Oscar Handlin, eds. *Harvard Encyclopedia of American Ethnic Groups.* London: The Belknap Press of Harvard University Press, 1981.

Wayne State University Department of Sociology and Anthropology. *Ethnic Groups in Detroit: 1951.* Detroit, MI: Wayne State University Department of Sociology and Anthropology, 1951.

Weiss, Bernard J., ed. *American Education and the European Immigrant, 1840-1940.* Urbana: University of Illinois Press, 1982.

Yakes, Daniel and Hugh Hornstein. *Muskegon First Hand.* Unpublished. Hockley Library, Muskegon, MI.

Icelanders

Arnbjörnsdóttir, Birna. *North American Icelandic: The Life of a Language.* Winnipeg: University of Manitoba Press, 2006.

Barrett, James H., ed. *Contact, Continuity, and Collapse: The Norse Colonization of the North Atlantic.* Turnhout, Belgium: Brepols Publishers, 2003.

Björnson, Valdimar. "Icelanders." In *Harvard Encyclopedia of American Ethnic Groups*, eds. Stephan Thernstrom, Ann Orlov, and Oscar Handlin. Cambridge, MA: Harvard University Press, 1980, pp. 474-476.

———. "Icelanders in the United States." *Scandinavian Review* 64 (1976): 39-41.

Byock, Jesse. *Viking Age Iceland.* New York: Penguin, 2001.

Eaton, Conan Bryant. "From Eyrarbakki to Muskegon: An Icelandic Saga," *Michigan History Magazine* 66, May/June 1982, 13-15.

———. *Washington Island: 1836-1876: A Part of the History of Washington Township.*

Washington Island, WI: Privately Published, 1980.

Einarsson, Bjarni F. *The Settlement of Iceland: A Critical Approach. Granastaðir and the Ecological Heritage*. Reykjavík, Iceland: Hið Íslenska bókmenntafélag, 1995.

Hall, Richard. *The World of the Vikings*. New York: Thames & Hudson, 2007.

Jonasson, Eric. *Tracing Your Icelandic Family Tree*. Winnipeg: Wheatfield Press, 1975.

Jones, Gwyn. *The Norse Atlantic Saga: Being the Norse Voyages of Discovery and Settlement to Iceland, Greenland, and North America*. 2nd ed. New York: Oxford University Press, 1986.

Lacy, Terry G. *Ring of Seasons, Iceland: Its Culture and History*. Ann Arbor: University of Michigan Press, 2000.

Magnaghi, Russell. "Icelanders on Washington Island, Wisconsin," *Preview* 5:12 (December 1985): 12–13.

Simundsson, Elva and Nelson Gerrard. *Icelandic Settlers in America*. Winnipeg, Manitoba: Queenston House, 1981.

Thor, Jonas. *Icelanders in North America: The First Settlers*. Winnipeg: University of Manitoba Press, 2002.

Thordarson, T. and G. Larsen. "Volcanism in Iceland in Historical Time: Volcano Types, Eruption Styles and Eruptive History." *Journal of Geodynamics* 43:1 (2007): 118–152.

Thorsteinsson, Thorsteinn and Tryggvi Oleson. *Saga Islendinga I Vesturheimi* (Saga of Icelanders in the Western World), 5 vols. Winnipeg and Reykjavik, 1940–1953.

Vasey, Daniel E. "Population Regulation, Ecology, and Political Economy in Preindustrial Iceland." *American Ethnologist* 23:2 (October 2009): 366–392.

Walters, Thorstina J. *Modern Sagas: The Story of Icelanders in North America*. Fargo, ND: 1953.

Index